I0571653

JOURNEY to AMERICA

AZEEZ AKANDE

JOURNEY TO AMERICA

THE STORY OF A YOUNG AFRICAN BOY WHO OVERCAME POVERTY AND ADVERSITY TO ATTAIN THE AMERICAN DREAM

A Memoir (Volume 1)

AZEEZ AKANDE

Library of Congress Cataloging-in-Publication Data
Names: Azeez Akande, author
Title: Journey to America / Azeez Akande
Identifiers: LCCN: 2024905483 /
(eBook) / ISBN: 9798990265516 /
(Paperback) / ISBN: 9798990265509 /
(Hardcover) / ISBN: 9798990265523

Published by

PRESTIGE PUBLISHERS
LIMITED

Prestigepublishersltd@gmail.com
+23491 5568 4563

Table of Contents

"

It ain't the size of the dog in the fight; it's the size of the fight in the dog.

– Mark Twain

"

Chapter One

Chasing the American Dream

People pointed and shouted at something I couldn't see. A flurry of excitement had taken over the usually quiet, dirty road leading to my best friend's house. The scene was filled with excitement as people were pointing, shouting, cheering, clapping, and singing, and dust was flying everywhere. I moved closer, pushing past those who blocked my view. As the crowd gradually dispersed, I caught a glimpse of a striking man standing in the middle of the crowd, wearing sunglasses, dark blue jeans, and a shirt with the word "YANKEES" printed on it. His white shoes were a stark contrast to the dust-covered surroundings; he looked dashing, and his stance commanded colossal admiration and respect. Children flocked around him, each vying for his attention; someone shouted that he had just returned from America.

My eyes lit up as the American man began to give out money and gifts to the villagers. Everyone was hugging each other. The atmosphere was clearly jubilant, and naked village boys jumped up and down in their excitement. Everyone was in awe. It was like the first coming of black Jesus Christ. Amidst the unhealthy and miserable conditions of our village, I couldn't help but wonder what he was doing there. He seemed like a god to everyone in our community. Being in the presence of the only man who had been to the white man's country made me happy. The only one among fifty thousand people who had been on a plane. He was the only black man on earth who had seen white people. For sure! America only consisted of white people. Everybody knew that! The American man shared stories of his experience living in the white man's land, beautifully painting images of America in everyone's mind. I stood in awe of his appearance, trying to picture his stories. But his efforts to get the villagers to relate to his stories proved futile; their imaginations couldn't stretch that far because no one had been to America before except for him. While everyone in the village, young and old, was happy about the gift of chocolate from America, I was left inspired and had a growing desire to go to America one day.

For the first time, I had a dream that I believed would bring me happiness. I had a vivid imagination of America – a land of beautiful white people walking on clean streets, stunning mansions with twenty-four-seven power supply, restaurants with all-you-can-eat buffets, clean drinking water rushing out from the tap anytime you want – as much as you want, good roads without any litter or dirt, a land free from poverty, and toilets that people can sit on. I was sold on the idea that America was the greatest country on earth, and ever since I have been chasing the American dream with a deliciously euphoric feeling.

I wanted to smell America's white air, walk on America's white soil, talk the American way, touch the almighty American dollar, and, most importantly, have sex with a beautiful American girl. Wild, I know, but that was what my twelve-year-old self wanted.

Reality struck me hard. I realized I had to rush back home as soon as possible to avoid my mother's wrath. But how would a young African boy with no resources be able to travel all the way to America? How could a boy who couldn't even leave his village for a day manage to ac- complish such a feat? A black boy who has nev- er gone beyond a twelve-mile radius from Modakeke? The thought was daunting, yet the allure of America was irresistible. I put my hands on my face and rubbed them to wipe away the desire for a place that provided all the joys I wished for.

The thought of encountering something so foreign, so unknown, yet so enticing filled me with a mix of excitement and apprehension. How would I respond to meeting something completely foreign and unknown to me? A place that offered all the happiness I sought. The dream was so vivid and enticing, it was impossible to let go. The desire to reach it, to touch it, and to live the dream was profound.

Lost in my imagination and thoughts, I forgot I had spent too much time getting home. *Ah*, I felt a familiar touch on my shoulder. "Oh my God! My mother will kill me." **I exclaimed as I realized it was my mother's hand on my shoulder.**

"

God provides trees but doesn't make furniture. – T.D. Jakes

"

Chapter Two

A Tale of Discovery

"Imagine a life in the United States of America. Now, stop imagining and start acting. With Apple Choice Nigeria Limited, that dream can become a reality. It takes a daring heart to reach an unprecedented level of success. To turn your dreams into reality, pitch your tent with the reliable and trustworthy people of Apple Choice Nigeria Limited; they know the way to success without tears and will guide you every step of the way. You can succeed and be celebrated if you believe you can. You can turn your dreams, your child's dreams, and your family's dreams of moving to the United States of America into a reality. Start the process now. Stagnation is a disease; act fast, act now.

Apple Choice Nigeria Limited – turning dreams into reality, one success story at a time."

As I listened to the advertisement on the radio, every hair on my body stood up with joy and anticipation. I gazed at my father with so much expectation, hoping he would respond and say something to me about the jingle that had just played on the eight o'clock news.

"Daddy, can we travel to America?" I asked my father with hope in my eyes. "Daddy, have you ever thought about traveling out of Nigeria? Do you think it's difficult to travel to America?" I continued to inquire. "Daddy... with a small fee, Apple Choice promised that we could become U.S. citizens, where we could live forever," I tried to persuade my father, but he didn't respond.

The infomercial sounded too good to be ignored. But is it supposed to be this easy? Thoughts and questions flashed through my head as I listened alongside my father. It was as if the advertisement was directed primarily toward me because my father did not say a word. So, I managed to make myself unbothered and not question him too much. After managing to suppress my curiosity, my expectations crumbled as my father threw his face away while enjoying the night breeze and fanning himself with his old wooden hand fan. The stifling heat that filled the rooms inside our home seemed a world away as he basked in the cool, fresh air of the outdoors.

Days passed after the announcement of the American travel visa lottery, and I was still waiting for my father to say something while hoping he still remembered. The advertisement played on the radio every day from early October to November. My mind was completely consumed with thoughts of going to America. I couldn't stop thinking about it, not even for a moment. Why wouldn't I? My surroundings were peaceful and stable, providing me ample time to contemplate and nurture my dreams. I hoped my father would give me some feedback on my aspirations.

As the sun set on a beautiful Saturday summer evening, my father sat under the sprawling branches of a cashew tree, trying to catch some fresh air while escaping from the heat that filled the rooms inside. The gentle hum of his favorite radio station, 104.5 FM, provided a comforting soundtrack to his solitude while sitting in his favorite armchair. Once again, the air was filled with the catchy jingle of *"Make America Your New Home,"* a campaign by Apple Choice Nigeria Limited, the Choice of Champions. The advertisement, which played frequently on the radio, extended an enticing invitation to listeners to find their dream job in America. To my surprise, my father, who usually paid little attention to such advertisements, reached for a piece of paper. With a thoughtful expression on his face, he began to jot down the contact information broadcasted in the jingle. His actions, uncharacteristic and unexpected, added an element of intrigue to the otherwise serene evening.

Apple Choice Nigeria Limited, an immigration and travel consultant company, was our beacon of hope. They offered a service to help Nigerians file visa lottery paperwork with the U.S. government for a nominal fee. The day after hearing about the boundless opportunities a U.S. green card could offer, my father applied for the American visa lottery. The news filled me with an indescribable joy. It felt like we were one step closer to achieving my long-held dream; even though we had only just applied, it felt as if we had already won the lottery. I was brimming with expectations about a process I knew nothing about, but I was certain that life in the U.S.A. meant a world of opportunities, and the financial reward would justify the risk.

However, our dreams were met with disappointment year after year. We did not win the visa lottery in 2000, 2001, 2002, or 2003. Despite our persistent efforts, the lottery was never forthcoming. Hope began to dwindle as we heard of countless other people across the coun- try who, like us, applied for the American lot- tery but never won. The American dream began to feel more like a pipedream, a tantalizing illusion peddled by the travel agency. Yet, we held onto the sliver of hope, the possibility that one day, our number would be called, and our dreams would become reality.

Despite Nigeria's faltering economy, its citizens remained undeterred in their pursuit of the green card lottery, leading to Nigeria having the highest number of applicants each year. Annually, over a million individuals apply for a U.S. visa, but only a small percentage are chosen through a random lottery system.

It took five long years of attempts before the villagers learned about Mr. Suleiman, a lottery winner from 2004. His triumph instilled a new-found sense of hope and courage within the community, challenging the prevailing belief that the lottery was merely a tool for the city's affluent to amass wealth or a ploy to exploit the poor under the guise of the American dream. As we gained the courage to pursue the American visa lottery scheme, our hopes increased, and I reassured myself, "Everything will be alright. I can still make it to America. One day, I will set foot on that land." **I was certain of it.**

"

"African children must respectfully challenge the status quo within the African cultural context."

— Yaw Osei

"

Chapter Three

Allow Me to Introduce Myself

My name is Azeez Akande, a proud son of Africa, born and raised in a typical African household. My village was exactly how an American television ad would portray it – a place where children will die without your donations. *The ad might say you can help a needy African child for sixty-five cents a day or nineteen dollars a month.* In other words, a prosperous, helpful white person could spend a few cents a day and become a hero to one of the kids who grew up in my village. Like many African children, I bear the marks of my culture – two deep cuts etched on my cheeks, a symbol of the Yoruba tradition. The early years of my life were shrouded in mystery, as is true for most of us. Our lives are guided by the limited knowledge we possess, and we navigate our existence around this pivotal piece of information.

I hail from Modakeke in Osun State, Nigeria, a community known for its bravery in war and prosperity in farming. Yet, we were surrounded by barren lands and infertile grounds. Many children were denied the opportunity to attend the only school available to us, as they were needed on the farms to help their fathers grow cash crops and make ends meet.

My village has been embroiled in conflict for many years due to the infamous battle between Modakeke and our neighboring community, Ile-Ife. Despite these challenges, we continue to persevere, embodying the spirit of resilience that defines us.

The Ile-Ife and Modakeke conflict started as far back as the 18th century. It is the oldest intra-ethnic conflict in Nigeria. The most prominent causes of this strained relationship were the divergent views of these communities about land ownership, acquisition, and usage. Closely related to this was the issue of identity. Ile- Ife people perceived the demand for local autonomy by the people of Modakeke as a daydream that should never come to pass. To the Modakeke people, there was no rationale behind the Ile-Ife people referring to Modakeke as a quarter but as a town distinct from Ile-Ife. These beliefs caused occasional accusations and counter-accusations, culminating in communal clashes. As a result, the two communities could not get along.

From 1849 to 1950, the villages engaged in conflict three times. In the 1980s, there were some minor hostilities between April 1981 and July 1983, but they were nothing compared to what happened in the 1990s. The major conflict began in August 1997 and lasted until August 1998.

The hostilities that took place between

March 3 and July 5, 2000, were a result of the Modakeke people's ongoing desire for independence and autonomy. In order to address this issue, the federal government was urged to grant them a rightful local government where they could hold leadership positions and contribute significantly to the development of Modakeke's economy. The late Sani Abacha military junta granted their wish by creating Ife East Local Government out of the former Ife North and Central local governments. However, Ile-Ife indigenes wanted the new council headquarters to be located in their part of town, whereas the Modakeke people disagreed. The government initially promised that Oke D.O. in Modakeke would be the location but later announced Oke-Ogbo in Ile-Ife as the headquarters. This move was perceived as cheating and injustice by the Modakeke people, who swiftly protested. As a result, a full-blown war ensued.

The year 2000 saw no peace whatsoever.

Modakeke youths marched towards Ile-Ife territory armed with rocks, knives, charms, broken glass bottles, sticks, and machetes to protest the constant oppression of their community. However, they were quickly dispersed with tear gas canisters fired by armed policemen. This signaled the beginning of a new Ile-Ife-Modakeke War. By August 18, the police officers were outnumbered and outgunned; they took to their heels when they could not contain the fighting. As a result, the war that began with rocks ended with full-scale violence, and sophisticated weapons dominated the life of the crisis. The children of both communities watched in distress and anguish as their fathers, brothers, and uncles unleashed mayhem on each other.

Hundreds lost their lives, and properties worth millions of dollars were looted and destroyed in both regions. The effects of these wars were enormous. Ile-Ife people slaughtered their neighbors who had once been their dearest friends. Modakeke people maimed innocent infants born on the other side of town to their godchildren. Lack of security of life and property became the order of the day.

For over two hundred years, the neighboring communities of Ile-Ife and Modakeke have had strained relationships characterized by hostility, political upheavals, and warfare. Nevertheless, the two communities are united through business and marriage. Though they are considered in- laws, what people see outside their doors from both villages is the same. The house on the right is Ile-Ife, while sitting just a foot away is Modakeke. Ile-Ife and Modakeke share the same views but differ culturally and have distinct dialects of the Yoruba language.

After years of cultural conflict, there seems to be no clear victor. My village has undergone significant changes since the onset of these disputes; several kids like me never had opportunities for life's essential amenities such as clean *water supply, properly maintained roads, and 24/7 power supply.* In Modakeke, we lived in darkness from dusk to dawn. Open defecation was the norm; trash littered the streets, and a significant percentage of the children looked like they had been starving. The water we drank was so contaminated that it would not be fit for washing shoes in America. My village was where outsiders would ask if the people there wore clothes or walked around with a garment that barely covered our privates; they would ask if we had a lion as a pet and if the lion's teeth had made the tribal marks on our faces.

Growing up in Nigeria, I was exposed to a society where military dictators took turns at the highest level with military force, and seeing soldiers on the streets in their green khaki uni-forms was a common sight. "The military became involved with politics for the betterment of Nigeria," they said. Promising peace, economic stability, and good leadership.

However, our hopes for a strong military that would support us were shattered when we realized that the military dictators were corrupt and no different from the civilians they overthrew. We had no one to look up to, no one to respect and admire, as our people died in silence. We had no civil rights activists; no George Washington, no Abraham Lincoln, no Martin Luther King, Jr., no Jessie Jackson, or Barack Obama. All our leaders were international criminals who had diverted our communities' resources to the white man's land. They were only concerned with consolidating their power and sharing the national cake. Their minds were occupied with thoughts of how to take possession of the nation's wealth into their accounts.

Despite facing constant adversity, we found refuge in God. We firmly believed that God was the solution to all our problems. He will provide us with sustenance, and people say that the fear of God is the beginning of wisdom. We trusted that God was the only one capable of fixing our bad roads and that he was our guiding light in the darkness.

Religion holds a significant place in our lives and our identity in Africa. We were introduced to God early in school, where we were required to take Christian and Muslim Religious courses. We learned about how he was a good God from the numerous churches surrounding our homes, and we also couldn't avoid hearing the Muslim call to prayer recited five times a day from the overlapping loudspeakers on mosque minarets, a constant reminder of God's message. These teachings emphasized that God was benevolent, and Jesus embodied truth. I knew God was the source of everything that most societies accept as just, moral, and reasonable. So, when the electricity went out, I prayed to God to restore it. Praying to God was the only consolation I could give myself while hoping things would improve.

Growing up in Africa's complex, multicultural society, we did not have a standard education system. Nonetheless, the expectations were clear, and the mindset was highly traditional. Our parents wanted us to become doctors, pharmacists, lawyers, or engineers. Successfully becoming any of these professions is a generational breakthrough that automatically makes you celebrated in society. When I was younger, I dreamed of becoming a doctor, thinking it would surely make my father happy.

However, my dream changed **after I met the "American man."**

"

"The nations that do best are the ones that invest in the education of their people."

— Obama

"

Chapter Four

Behind the Counselor's Doors

The doors of our house never took a rest. *Gba, Gba, Gbam,* as visitors came and went through the doors. I could hear the doors constantly being shut, keeping the rhythms of our bustling home. Many of these visitors were students from the community who were preparing to take their senior year exams. Despite his tough exterior, my father, affectionately known as the "Counsellor," was always welcoming, and his doors were always open to his students. His reputation as a man of integrity and wisdom preceded him, making him a respected figure in Modakeke. He was not just the head of our household, but also a guiding light for many seeking advice on politics or education.

My father's realm of influence extended to Modakeke High School, my alma mater, where he taught social studies and later became the guidance counselor. He was a mentor to the students, helping them develop ideas for examination questions and their solutions. He also took the opportunity to educate students on ethics, morals, and other topics related to career development that would interest a teenager at that time. His influence was so profound that everyone at the school knew me, not for any personal achievement, but simply because I was the counselor's son.

My father was a strict and conscientious person who never allowed familial ties to influence his personal conduct. At school, I was treated no differently than any other student. But at home, the expectations were high. I was expected to put in extra effort, to strive for excellence. This dichotomy of experiences, of being just another student at school and the counselor's son at home shaped my character and taught me valuable lessons about fairness, hard work, and the pursuit of knowledge.

Growing up as the son of the school counselor, I was under the constant scrutiny of high expectations, and it seemed like everyone in school did, too. I could understand why. My father led by example, and everyone expected his son to follow suit. I still remember the sting of disappointment in my math teacher's eyes when I failed to complete an assignment, a punishment that felt more severe due to the weight of the unspoken expectations.

At home, love and care were abundant, but they came with a strict set of social rules. The African culture I was raised in held respect for elders in high regard. Standing while an elder was seated or sitting while they stood could invite reprimands. Expressing emotions was a tightrope walk – crying out of pain could be seen as being overly emotional, while not crying could be interpreted as not feeling enough pain. It was a confusing and often an unfair balancing act.

In Africa, it's not uncommon for a child to be disciplined and then told not to cry. As a child, I wasn't allowed to express disapproval towards my parents, and my opinions didn't matter. I was expected to follow their rules without questions. Only the children of wealthy parents were fortunate enough to have permissive parents who indulged their every whim. For the average Nigerian parent, discipline meant keeping a koboko, a long, thick cane with a scattered and extended tip, in the back corner of their living room. Just a single stroke of this cane was enough to make a child gentle and obedient for the rest of the week. Although it was extremely painful, many parents believed it was necessary for a child's upbringing. In fact, Nigerian parents who did not beat or punish their children were often considered to have failed in their parenting, regardless of how obedient their children were.

When I first heard about parenting practices in America, I was taken aback. I learned that American parents often apologize to their children when they make a mistake or reprimand them unjustly. American children are encouraged to assert their rights, and they can even seek law enforcement intervention if they feel mistreated. This was a stark contrast to my upbringing in Nigeria.

In our African culture, elders were always right, and challenging this notion was considered a taboo. Consequently, accusing my father of falsehood, even when he was wrong, was out of the question. There was no recourse if my father was unjust; not even my mother could intervene, as they presented a united front. I yearned for the freedom I perceived in America, where I could engage in activities I enjoyed without the fear of unwarranted reprimands or punishments from my parents. The narratives shared by the American dad **fueled my desire to experience life in America.**

66

"It's not the people who vote that count. It's the people who count the votes."

— Joseph Stalin

99

Chapter Five

Steering Osun State Towards a Scientific Future

His Excellency, Chief Bisi Akande, ex-governor of Osun State, made a significant move to revamp the state's not-so-good education system when he took office in 1999. His administration made the bold decision to lay off 23,000 public servants, including 4,000 teachers, particularly those specializing in liberal arts and other creative fields. This decision came as a surprise to many, as people expected the government to focus on training and retraining the teachers. Instead, the governor opted to convert all Osun State schools into science-focused institutions that emphasized subjects like English language, mathematics, physics, chemistry, biology, and other essential fields that would produce future doctors, lawyers, and engineers.

The repercussions of the mass layoffs were felt throughout Osun State. Restaurants closed, newspaper stands were empty, markets turned into ghost towns, and transport workers found themselves without passengers. The situation was particularly dire in Modakeke, a town still recovering from previous community crises with Ile-Ife. As a result of the job losses, many marriages were strained, careers were disrupted, and dreams were shattered. Countless unemployed teachers were struggling to cope, and some civil servants even took their own lives because they could no longer provide for their families. The chaos and unrest were widespread throughout the state, and it seemed that there was no end in sight.

Chief Bisi Akande stated that when Osun State was created in 1991, it inherited a large workforce, many of whom were unproductive and unnecessary. During that period, there was a prevailing notion that vocational and liberal arts studies had become obsolete, and that the future lay solely in the realm of science education. The governor's decision to terminate a large number of teachers in one fell swoop seemed like a bold, strategic move to downsize the workforce. However, this decision had unintended consequences that were not initially apparent.

The labels that were casually thrown around to justify the layoffs were not just impersonal categories. They were attached to real people who were integral parts of our community. The so-called "useless teachers" were, in fact, the fathers of my friends, shaping young minds and guiding us through our formative years. The "parasites" were my mother's friends; women who dedicated their lives to public service and contributed to our society. And among the "deadwoods" was my own father, a man who, despite the label, was anything but unproductive or unnecessary. These dismissive labels failed to capture the value these individuals brought to our community and the impact they had on our lives. The personal cost of these layoffs was much more than what was acknowledged in the public discourse. It was a stark reminder that behind every policy decision, there are real people whose lives are profoundly affected. In the face of adversity, my father took decisive action to prevent our family from succumbing to starvation. On a sun-drenched afternoon, I found myself walking down the road, a hoe resting on my left shoulder and a cutlass in my right hand. The day had already been spent assisting my mother with the morning chores, and now I was rushing to join my father on his farmland.

In Nigeria, farming is often viewed as a menial job, a last resort for the impoverished. Yet, my father was undeterred by this societal perception. He traded his pens and papers for cutlasses and hoes, transforming himself from a white-collar worker to a farmer. He meticulously planted thirty rows of corn, twenty rows of cassava, ten rows of yam tubers, an assortment of vegetables, and fifty banana trees from seed. My father's resilience was a testament to his character. He didn't allow societal opinions to dissuade him from his path. Instead, he persevered, demonstrating a willingness to learn and adapt. His efforts ensured our family's survival, providing us with sustenance despite the challenging circumstances.

I wondered if there were farmlands in America and, if so, who would be planting and harvesting the crops. Perhaps Americans are too wealthy to work on farms, I mused. However, I was getting distracted from the reality of my own life.

In the wake of the changes in the school system, I found myself reflecting on my father's contributions to the school and the community. His absence was deeply felt, and his impact became even more apparent. I developed a new-found appreciation for teachers worldwide, irrespective of the subjects they taught. I witnessed numerous teachers who poured their heart and soul into their work, often with little recognition or reward.

The primary responsibility of any government is to safeguard the welfare of its citizens. However, within three years, there was a disturbing increase in the number of suicides in the state. Despite this, Governor Chief Bisi Akande announced his candidacy for re-election.

His campaign advertisements were being broadcast on the radio 24/7. The ads urged people to vote for him, citing his political sagacity, moral integrity, and financial prudence. However, it was somewhat comical that the same governor, whose first term was marked by a lack of competence and poor crisis management, sought another term in office. His tenure had seen the education system undergo drastic changes, leading to job losses and a decline in the quality of education. The disconnect between his campaign promises and the reality on the ground was stark. Despite being ineligible to vote, I felt a strong sense of civic duty. Fueled by my father's dismissal and my own experiences working on the farm, I campaigned door-to-door, advocating for a change in leadership.

In contrast, the People's Democratic Party (PDP) nominated Olagunsoye Oyinlola, a retired Nigerian Army member, for the governorship position. His promise to reinstate all the dismissed teachers if elected garnered him substantial support, particularly from civil servants who had been laid off by Governor Akande. The election day, Saturday, April 19, 2003, was a day fraught with tension. The state of Osun was abuzz with anticipation and anxiety. Opinions were divided, and millions turned out to cast their votes. Some believed that the incumbent governor would leverage his power to secure a victory, while others were confident that the citizens of Osun State would ensure he was not re-elected. Despite the widespread desire for change, there was a palpable fear of potential election rigging.

As the day wore on, rumors began to circulate about the governor's surrogates giving away bags of rice adorned with his face in exchange for votes. This tactic, a direct handout to sway voters, is a common practice among politicians in Nigeria to woo voters and secure victory. As the sun set on this pivotal day, the fate of Osun State hung in the balance, and the outcome of the election had yet to be determined.

The relationship between Nigerian voters and their elected officials can be likened to the allegory of the Soviet dictator, Joseph Stalin, and his chicken. Stalin, demonstrated a brutal lesson in power dynamics by plucking a live chicken bare, causing it immense pain, only to have the chicken follow him for food. This story serves as a metaphor for the relationship between the people of Osun State and their elected officials. The people, represented by the chicken, endure hardship and suffering, yet they follow those who offer them sustenance, even if it is the same hand that caused their pain.

This analogy is particularly poignant in the context of the Osun State elections. The people, having endured hardship under the incumbent governor, were desperate for relief. The promise of a bag of rice was enough to sway their allegiance, turning the giver into a deity.

After a tense twelve-hour ballot count, the fear and anticipation were palpable. The clock on the wall seemed to tick louder with each passing second; the realization that our lives were intrinsically linked to the election outcome was sobering. Our future was hanging in the balance, hinging on the outcome of this election. The prospect of the incumbent governor's re-election was daunting.

As I sat next to my father, his gaze was fixated on the radio, our only source of information. "We have the final results," the radio presenter announced. My heart pounded in my chest as we leaned forward, our breaths held in anticipation. The moment we had been waiting for was finally here.

The new governor-elect is Chief Olagunsoye Oyinlola, the candidate of the People's Democratic Party (PDP).

Anxiety gave way to elation. Joy filled our hearts as the news sank in. It felt as though a weight had been lifted, and smiles returned to our faces. As we celebrated this historic event, I couldn't help but feel a sense of pride. Pride in our state, in our people, and in the democratic process, a significant shift in Osun State's history. It was indeed an event not to be forgotten, **a moment forever etched in the annals of our state's history.**

66

"International loans can be worse than the slave trade."

— Bisi Akande

99

Chapter Six

Voyage to the New World

It was very late in the middle of the night, and I was fast asleep in the realm of dreams when suddenly, a strange noise echoed loudly from the living room. My peace was interrupted as I tossed and turned in bed, wondering what was going on. It was my father who was making the noise at almost midnight, I soon discovered. I got up and walked towards the living room, barely able to keep my eyes open. The noise amplifying with each step. Upon entering, my gaze fell upon a familiar sight – a brown envelope lying hopelessly on the floor with my father's name on it. I immediately knew what it was; it was a letter from the American visa lottery.

My father applied for a U.S.A. visa through the visa lottery program for four consecutive years, only to be rejected each time. These rejection letters always came in a brown envelope.

I watched my father open and toss one of these brown envelopes across the room a year ago. He had done the same thing two years before that. I witnessed my father, year after year, open these envelopes and toss them aside in disappointment. His face turned to a frown; his mind lost in deep thoughts as he read the disheartening contents of the letter. Each one began with a courteous "Thank you for applying for the American visa lottery," only to be followed by the bad news that his application had not been randomly selected for processing by the U.S. Citizenship and Immigration Services.

Every year, my father anxiously awaited the results, hoping he would be a visa lottery winner. Instead, he would desperately stare at terrible news we could do nothing about.

The sight of these brown envelopes had become a painful reminder of our unattained dream. He would shake his head, knowing he would have to listen to another year of paid ads by visa lottery agencies, screaming, "Do not miss your chance; apply today and be one of the next lucky green card winners."

This year was no different. My father had the same look on his face as he opened the brown envelope. I looked to his side to find my mother and siblings, who had awakened earlier than I had from all the noise. Their faces didn't look good, maybe because they also just woke up from sleep and were still trying to grasp what was happening. However, I had already grown accustomed to thinking and making assumptions in my head. I was sure it wasn't a piece of good news this time, either.

With a deep breath that seemed to carry the weight of our collective anticipation, my father handed me the letter. "Son, read this," he said, his voice steady. The first word I saw in bold letters was **"*Congratulations*!"** "Oh my God," was the second thing that came out of my mouth after "Thank you, Baba God ... thank you, Jesus. ..." In a fit of joy, I tossed the paper into the air, like a rapper throwing money to strippers, madly screaming, fist-pumping, and showing all my thirty-two teeth with a big smile. The joy was infectious, impossible to contain. I jumped on the person next to me, not caring whether it was my mother or my sister. We all hopped on each other and screamed in a chaotic symphony of happiness, all except my father, who watched the scene with a quiet sense of satisfaction. We didn't care what time of the night it was or whether our screams disturbed the sleep of our neighbors. This is our moment, a moment of triumph. Visions of a brighter future danced in my mind. The endless possibilities that awaited us in America filled my heart with excitement.

"Boy, you better pick the letter up," my father

chucked, his eyes twinkling with a hint of mischief. I sprang into action, scooping up the paper like a stripper picking up her money after a show-stopping performance. The words on the paper danced before my eyes, *"You are among those randomly selected and registered for further consideration in the DV-2003/ 2004 diversity immigration program for 2003 (October 1, 2002, to September 30, 2003)."*

Another surge of joy washed over me again. "Oh, yes, yes, yes ... our lives, filled with poverty and hopelessness, are about to change. No more living in this house overrun by rats and roaches. Soon, we will be living in America!" The thought was intoxicating, a promise of a better life just within our reach. The endless possibilities that awaited us in America filled my heart with excitement.

However, I couldn't help noticing the last paragraph. The words seemed to leap off the page, *"Selection does not guarantee that you will receive a visa; applicants selected are greater than the number of visas available."*

A frown creased my forehead as I read the sentence aloud, "I just ... I don't understand this," I confessed to my father. The jubilation that had lit up my face moments ago gradually faded, replaced by a look of confusion and concern. The reality of the situation began to sink in — our journey was far from over, and there were still hurdles to overcome. But we were one step closer, and that in itself was a victory worth celebrating.

It was already daybreak, the echoes of the midnight excitement still reverberated within me. Sleep had been elusive, the thrill of the news keeping me wide awake. I stepped outside, and looked up at the sky. It was no longer a limit but a path to our dream destination. The country we aspired to reach was known as God's own country, a land of prosperity and opportunity, where people enjoyed the benefits of government welfare and found dollars on the street. A country where jobs were abundant, with few applicants to compete against.

I breathed in the aroma from the kitchen; the food that morning must have felt my mother's happiness. It was as if her joy had infused the food, adding an extra layer of flavor that made it taste like a celebration. However, the thought of being selected but not granted the visa was daunting. The disappointment would be too much to bear. Yet, I clung to the hope that if we were granted the visa and made it to America, our lives would change for the better. We would never be the same again. **This was our chance, our opportunity to turn our dreams into reality, and we were ready to seize it.**

"

"When a black man comes to America, the first person he hates is the person who looks like him."

— Anonymous

"

Chapter Seven

Bridging Continents

Are we going to secure a signed affidavit of support requested by the U.S. embassy? Will our efforts go to waste? Will I lose this opportunity? I became more anxious as I remembered we had a limited time to pass a medical exam, undergo a background check, and find a U.S. sponsor with their most recent federal income tax papers and affidavit of support. Each tick of the clock is a constant reminder of the race against time we were in.

"You have reached the voicemail box of 908-689- 1234; please record your voice message at the tone. When you've finished recording, you may hang up or press pound for more options." The voice of a lady on the other end filled the room carefully pronounced each word after a week of my father's unanswered phone calls to Mr. Matthew, his old university friend who now resided in New Jersey. Each time the phone rang, it was picked up by a woman's voice. "Hello? Can you hear me?" my father would ask, only to be met with silence. The unanswered calls and the unfamiliar voice on the other end of the line raised many questions: Who was the white woman talking on Mr. Mathew's phone? Had we dialed the wrong number? Or had he married an American woman while his wife and kids were still in Nigeria? It took several attempts to realize that the voice belonged to a machine, not a person.

Repeatedly, my father persisted in his calls, unwavering in his determination. Each time the phone rang, he left brief yet heartfelt messages detailing his visa lottery win. He often pondered whether Mr. Matthew truly listened to these messages or if they were simply overlooked amidst the demands of adulthood. Yet, on one overcast afternoon, the phone rang. My father's heart leaped with anticipation. Grasping the receiver, his pulse quickened. "Hello?" he uttered. A moment of silence ensued, then a familiar voice echoed through the line, "Is this SK?" Tears blurred my father's vision as he choked out, "Matthew?" "Yes," came the reply. "It's been too long." Their conversation unfolded like that of old souls finding each other once more. In those moments, the years dissolved, leaving behind only the laughter lines etched around their eyes.

In the few conversations my father eventually had with Mr. Matthew, he often spoke about the challenges of living in America, a country of bills, how it pays well but collects everything with the other hand. "Imagine paying bills with 95% of your income," he would say. According to him, living in America is very difficult, yet he never expressed a desire to return to Nigeria.

My father would laugh, but Mr. Matthew did not mean what he said as a joke. I remember overhearing a conversation between him and my father. He spoke about how the U.S. economy is designed to extract wealth from its citizens. He believed that the system was designed to enslave Black people financially and that it makes sure they continue to owe the masters, just like they did the enslaved people. However, when someone beats the system and becomes wealthy, they call it the American Dream. He believed that the government promotes this idea to keep everyone in an endless pursuit of an elusive dream while enriching the top one percent.

Every word that fell from Mr. Matthew's mouth sounded more like a warning than advice. It's like warning a prisoner against finding its way out of captivity. His descriptions of life in America were stark, a contrast to the dream we had been nurturing. Yet, the last time he visited Nigeria, he was the embodiment of the American

Dream. He returned a millionaire with a sleek black Volvo S60 sedan and gifts of American candies and chocolates. His New York baseball cap and white shirt emblazoned with the word "YANKEES" became symbols of his success. He was the "American dad," the man who had made it, the man everyone admired. "The man" who painted America as a paradise, a land of opportunity and prosperity. His stories were captivating, making me fall in love with a place I had never seen. I could almost feel the vibrancy of life in America, the promise of a better future. He was the man that a huge crowd gathered around on a dusty clay road, who ignited my dreams of going to America, the man I aspired to be.

However, his conversation with my father revealed a different side of America. He spoke of the struggles Black people faced and the challenges that came with living in a foreign land. He cautioned my father against making hasty decisions, reminding us that the American Dream was not always as it seemed, a development that had added a layer of mystery to our interactions with him.

It is far easier to keep others from reaching the top when you are already there. Perhaps that's what American dad is doing; he was now saying that America is not easy having reached the top. His words now painted a picture of too much work, too much tax, too much stress, and Africans in America are confined to hard labor. Yet, he stayed there. I wondered where all the advice came from as I leaned in to listen carefully. I know that no country is perfect, and his words were a reminder that every dream comes with its own set of challenges, and that achieving it requires perseverance and resilience, but it is strange to hear someone who used to make America look like a paradise suddenly talk about how horrible it is to live there. His hesitation to take in my father and me was understandable. Providing for two additional people without proper planning could indeed be a challenge. After a lengthy conversation, Mr. Matthew couldn't offer much help besides his support and encouragement.

That's what friends do, they stand by each other through thick and thin.

Two months had passed since my father, and I received our visas from the U.S. consular office, and we knew that we would be leaving Nigeria soon. The reality of our impending departure from Nigeria was beginning to sink in.

My father penned an email to Mr. Matthew, expressing our gratitude for his support. We wished him nothing but blessings and financial prosperity from God, **a small token of our appreciation for everything he had done for us.**

"

"The whole object of travel is not to set foot on foreign land; it is at last to set foot on one's own country as a foreign land."

— G. K. Chetsterton

"

Chapter Eight

From Humble Beginnings to New Horizons

I watched the clock tick away, one, two, three, until morning broke. I found myself wide awake and heard the insects outside my window all night long. At four o'clock, I got up, went outside, and took one last poop in the bush. I knew that my next bowel movement would be in a high-efficiency dual-flush elongated toilet. A far cry from the bush I was accustomed to. The morning was hot and humid, the air thick with anticipation. My mother held me tightly in her embrace and pleaded with me not to forget her. We were both overcome with emotion, and I couldn't help but feel a mix of nervousness and excitement for the new chapter that lay ahead. I dreaded leaving my mother behind with tears in her eyes. Her words, *"Ranti omo e ni ton se o,"* echoed in my ears, as she hugged me tightly, begging me not to forget her. Finally, the day I had been waiting for had arrived.

"I'll never forget you, Mom," I assured her, trying to ease her worries. My mother didn't feel excited about losing her first son until God knows when. "I'll be sending you money," I comforted her.

Her tears had been a constant companion over the past twenty-four hours, a testament to the depth of her love and concern. She cried during breakfast, while making dinner, and every other moment in between. She knew that in a few hours, there would be nothing she could do to help me from a faraway land. She packed my clothes in a 'Ghana Must Go' bag, along with many other things I couldn't find in America, like garri, egusi, kulikuli, iru, elubo, alligator pepper, bitter leaf, dried croaker fish, and kpekere.

As the hour of departure drew near — less than two hours before I bade the village goodbye and boarded an airplane for the first time, I felt a pang of sadness. Leaving behind my familiar surroundings and my mother was not easy. I could see the mix of emotions on her face too — joy for my adventure, but also worry as any mother would feel when sending her son to a faraway land that she can't easily reach. She stared at my father as the expression, *take good care of my son,* filled her face. I hugged my mother one last time, and wished her good health before my father and I snuck out of the house, into an awaiting taxi.

We had to be discreet to avoid the attention of the villagers. If word got out that we were leaving for America, the whole village would have come to our house to wave us goodbye and turn farewell into a day-long celebration. So, I ducked down in the back seat, covered with my mother's African fabrics, while my father sat in the front passenger seat as if he was taking a taxi like any other day.

As we drove away, I couldn't help but look back one last time. This was not a goodbye, but a promise of a better future. A promise that I intended to keep.

"Park, Park, Park. Park very well!" Every eye in the car turned to the man in the black police uniform waving an AK-47 rifle in the middle of the road, commanding our attention. "What in God's name is going on?" I asked, though the answer was already clear. Police roadblocks were a common sight on Nigerian roads, an unfortunate reality for everyday road users. Mr. Habib, our taxi driver, complied, pulling over to the side of the road. Fear gripped me, and my brain was on alert for danger as I took in the sight of the uniformed shooters lining the half-asphalt, half-dust road of the Ile-Ife to Ibadan expressway. Despite the danger, this was just the way things were in the country and everyone had come to accept it.

"Wey your particulars?" one of the police officers demanded, his face stern, his hand hovering over his gun as if ready to shoot at any moment. His demeanor was intimidating, and I thought he would not let us go quickly. My father and I sat silently; we knew our lips would not change a thing. We must comply with whatever they say to avoid unnecessary delays.

"Oga, I get all my papers o, see my road worthiness paper, oga check my fire extinguisher and its receipt ... "

"Open your boot," another officer commanded the taxi driver. As the officers rummaged through our belongings in the trunk, another officer approached us. His deep voice cut through the loud noise of passing motorists blasting their horns, alerting street hawkers selling newspapers, bread, and pure water in the middle of the road to get out of the way. "Oya make you no dey dull now. You kno say police na your friend ..." I grinned to myself. This is the language police use to turn checkpoints into lucrative criminal ventures and demand bribes from drivers and passengers. I wasn't sure if I agreed with the police's last statement, the driver didn't either, as the expression on his face gave him away.

"Oga, I've shown you all my particulars. You don see the boot, oga make I dey go, please," our taxi driver pleaded with the officers, but his pleas fell on deaf ears. "Leave those talks ... give us something for the weekend." The unspoken threat hung in the air—comply or face the consequences.

Knowing the potential repercussions of non-compliance, the taxi driver would be detained and harassed, and the police would tow the taxi to the nearest station for a more thorough search until payment was negotiated for its release. This would leave us stranded; my father reached out and handed the officer five hundred naira.

It was a small price to pay to avoid any mishaps and ensure our journey continued without any further delays.

Just after seven o'clock pm, when we passed by a towering twelve-foot statue of three Lagos chiefs, a sign reading '*Welcome to Lagos, the Centre of Excellence*' stood proudly beside it. After that, the freeway turned into a chaotic dance of weaving and braking, transforming our three-hour commute into a six-hour or- deal. Pedestrians and taxi drivers jostled for space on the infamous road. No one was waiting for anyone, and everyone wanted to move simultaneously. This was a common sight in Lagos, a city that never slept, but for us villagers, it was a stark contrast to the tranquility we were accustomed to.

We arrived at the Murtala International Airport with sweat dripping down our backs. I couldn't tell if it was from the hot, humid weather or the stress of walking with tired steps through hundreds of people who crowded the terminal. The airport was bustling with activity, with many people begging for money than passengers boarding planes.

An immigration officer approached us, offering to expedite the process of stamping our passports. Her request for 'breakfast' money was met with disbelief, "Madam, which kind of breakfast at 9:25 pm?" I replied. "You con dey argue, or you con dey go to America?" she asked.

I knew better than to argue. A swift exchange of two thousand naira ensured our passage to the full-body scanner.

The security check was a flurry of activity. Shoes off, belt off, empty pockets—the orders were barked out in quick succession. "Boss, what's in this pocket?" A pat-down revealed some Nigerian currencies in my chest pocket, which I handed over without protest.

As I made the long left turn to the airport corridor, I couldn't help but stare at the band of runaways who probably shared my desire for a better life in a white man's country. This was the moment I had been waiting for, the culmination of years of dreams and aspirations. I turned to my father, a smile on my face and a whisper on my lips, **"My dream is here; I'm finally going to America."**

"

The biggest addiction a person can have is discovering the unknown.

— Stephen Backpacker's Tale

"

Chapter Nine

First Glimpse of America

Is this reality or just a dream? I had envisioned this moment countless times, but seeing everything in person brought me so much joy that all I could do was stare in admiration. The flight attendant ushered me to my seat, and I couldn't help but absorb every detail of my surroundings. The clouds outside the window were thick and beautiful, and everything below seemed so small and insignificant. I couldn't help but exclaim, "Wow!" Seeing everything as I had imagined couldn't give me any less feeling. My expectations were more dramatic than the reality of it all. The height of the plane didn't scare me; instead, it fascinated me. This was unlike the American dad's first flight experience, when he expressed his fear of heights. I doubted anyone else on that flight was as thrilled as I was. Yes, I was finally on my way to America.

Soaring at an altitude of 30,000 feet, I was handed a tray of food by the flight attendant. The tray was filled with an assortment of dishes: an entrée, a salad with dressing, sweet and sour beef with brown rice, quinoa, ice cream, and pretzels. This was my first encounter with Western cuisine, I decided to give it a try, eager to try white people's food for the first time.

The food was different, and the flavors were unfamiliar. It was nothing like the taste of my mother's home-cooked meals. Nonetheless, I took big bites, trying to experience as much of the new cuisine as possible. Unfortunately, my adventurous spirit was met with resistance from my stomach. The unfamiliar food didn't sit well, and I soon found myself feeling nauseous.

Before I knew it, I was overcome with sickness, and I ended up vomiting all over myself right there in my seat.

The foreign food had proven to be too much to handle. I cleaned myself up with a complimentary red blanket left on my seat, avoiding any unnecessary attention.

In the early morning hours, our plane touched down at Heathrow Airport for a brief stopover. As I peered out of the expansive glass windows that stretched from floor to ceiling, I was struck by the distinct and elegant beauty of the sky. I noticed that the sky looked different and refined. The Royal Botanic Gardens, visible in the distance, were stunning.

Inside the airport, the scene was unlike anything I had ever experienced. To my left, a lounge area was outfitted with rows of plush black leather chairs, with a fully equipped electronic charging station at its heart. To my right, restaurants bustled with white people, their faces lit up with smiles as they enjoyed their meals.

Heathrow Airport was a hive of activity. I watched as travelers embarked and disembarked from planes, and elevators moved people up and down between floors. As I navigated the labyrinthine corridors of this well-organized international hub, the sounds of fellow travelers bound for the United States filled the air, creating a symphony of anticipation and excitement.

After a journey that spanned sixteen hours and bridged two continents, my father and I finally arrived on American soil. It was four in the afternoon, a full day after we had bid farewell to our homeland, Nigeria.

Stepping off the plane and onto the stairs, the first thing that caught my eye was the American flag. Its bold red, white, and blue colors were displayed proudly everywhere I looked. From the stairs leading down from the plane, to the entrance of the customs and baggage claim area, the flag was a constant, welcoming presence.

As we made our way through the bustling terminal of Newark Liberty International Airport, the flag continued to be a prominent sight. It was posted outside the exit gate at Terminal C, fluttering in the breeze. I spent most of the afternoon counting the white stars on the blue canton, the fields of alternating stripes, and the red and white lines on the American flag.

Stepping into the heart of America, oversized glass automated doors opened to the sight of expansive, well-paved roads stretching out before us. They led to impressive buildings, their gardens meticulously maintained, and the ever-present American flags fluttering proudly from houses and apartment windows.

In Africa, our homes didn't display our national flag. Yet here in America, the national colors were displayed with pride everywhere I looked. I didn't fully understand why but seeing them stirred a sense of allegiance within me. I felt a newfound respect for the flag and a desire to honor it, as it was a symbol of my new home.

Since coming to America, my emotions had been a whirlwind. There was a sense of relief that was hard to ignore. Gone are the days when I would wake up each morning, praying for the electricity to come on. I no longer had to fetch water from a hole dug in the sand nor clean up after the free-range animals in the compound. The daily chores of a long walk to fetch onions and peppers from the "better life" market for my mother's jollof rice were now a thing of the past. And the constant vigilance for rain clouds, hoping to avoid the long trek to fetch water, was no longer necessary.

As the days switched into weeks, the Jerry Springer show became my unofficial English language class, where I would echo every word, trying to mimic the pronunciation as accurately as possible. I found myself gradually adapting to the American way of life. I began to understand the nuances of their speech and interactions. I even learned three essential American words: bitch, slut, and whore. All this while savoring a unique concoction of orange juice with a hint of milk. "Ya know what I'm saying," became my catchphrase.

Back home, news of my journey to America had spread like wildfire. My mother, now seven thousand miles away from her son, had become the center of attention. My father was inundated with messages from villagers expressing their displeasure at not being informed about our visa lottery success. I could empathize with their feelings of discontent. It was a reminder of the close-knit community I had left behind, even as I was embracing my new life in America.

A month into my American journey, I found myself at the Department of Motor Vehicles (DMV) on Route 31 North in New Jersey. The goal was to obtain a driver's license, a necessary step to legally drive in the state.

I had been warned about the potential

challenges at the DMV, tales of seemingly simple tasks turning into enormous trials filled with frustration. Undeterred, I approached the customer service representative at the front desk, greeting her with a cheerful "Good morning." Donning a shirt in green-white-green, the colors of my Nigerian homeland.

She asked how she could assist me, and I responded, "My name is Akande Azeez Adesola, and I am here for my computer road test." My words, spoken with my African accent, seemed to puzzle her. She asked for my ID, and I shook my head, indicating I didn't have one.

"What did you say your name is again?" she asked. As I repeated my name, her confusion seemed to deepen. I could feel the weight of her gaze on me, her curiosity piqued by my accent and the foreignness of my name. She asked me to spell it out, and I began to spell my last name first, "A-K-A-N-..." She interrupted me, asking me to spell it slower, using examples like "A for apple. "I complied, starting again with "A as in apple."

When I got to "K," the second letter of my first name. I used "kangaroo" as my example. This seemed to throw her off.

"K as in kangaroo"

"What?" she sneered.

"Kangaroo, K for kangaroo, K as in kangaroo," my voice filled the room.

She met my gaze once again, her eyes probing as if searching for something beyond my comprehension. I stood there, a mix of confusion and embarrassment washing over me. Fear gripped me as I struggled to understand what was happening. Suddenly, she reached for the phone on her desk. "Tom," she spoke into the receiver, "I need you up front." With that, she hung up, shook her head, and turned back to me. "Would you please step aside?" she asked, her tone firm yet not unkind. "Someone will be here shortly to assist you further."

As I stepped aside, I took a deep breath, steadying my racing heart. I didn't know what was coming next, but I knew I had to face it head-on.

"Right this way, sir," a voice echoed behind me. I turned to see Tom, dressed in a crisp black suit and a red tie. He looked every bit professional. I handed him my green card and social security card as he led me to his office. My gaze wandered to the portraits of George Bush and the state governor, Jim McGreevey, adorning the office walls. "She said you didn't have any I.D., but this card is your I.D.," he said, holding up my green card. I chuckled nervously, not knowing what to say. I hadn't realized that my green card and social security card could serve as identification.

"Well, Mr. Akande, did I say your name right?" Tom asked, reaching for a piece of paper from the printer. I nodded, appreciating his effort to pronounce my name correctly.

My eyes then drifted toward the computer room where I was supposed to take the test. The room was filled with rows of computers, each one glowing with an eerie blue light. It was a stark contrast to the warm and welcoming atmosphere of Tom's office. I had so many questions — about the test, about driving in America, about everything. But the memory of my previous encounter at the front desk held me back. I chose to remain silent, opting instead to observe and learn from my surroundings.

I was 18 years old when we landed in America. The small, cramped apartment at American Dad's place had been our refuge for six months. We found solace in his hospitality for those 6 months. However, as the days turned into weeks, and the weeks into months, the cracks in our harmonious coexistence began to show.

It started innocently. American dad would wake me up late at night, his face flushed with irritation. "Your breathing," he'd say, pointing his finger at me. "It's like a freight train. I'd apologize profusely, promising to breathe more quietly.

Then came the electricity bills. He would thrust them on the table, his eyebrows furrowed. "You're using too much light," he'd grumble. This bill is too much."

We'd nod, feeling guilty for the burden we unwittingly placed on him. We'd turn off lights, unplug appliances, and tiptoe around the apartment, hoping to appease our host. But the final blow came in the form of an eviction notice — a cold, impersonal letter slipped under the door.

"Dear Tenant,

We have noticed that you have two or more people living with you for the past six months. As clearly stated in the lease, no tenant is allowed to have visitors for more than a week. We will be terminating your tenancy and evicting you from the property in fifteen days if your visitors are found on the premises.

Thank you,

The Management"

My heart sank as I read those words. We were being cast out; our fragile stability shattered. Mr. Mathew, the man who'd once welcomed us, was now the harbinger of our displacement.

Desperation fueled my determination. I took extra shifts at work, scraped every penny I had saved up, and counted the days until our eviction. And then, on a rainy afternoon, we signed the lease for our own apartment—a one-bedroom space two doors from Mr. Matthew's studio apartment. **In our humble abode, my father and I began anew.**

"

"A mind that is stretched by a new experience can never go back to its old dimensions."

— Oliver Wendell Homes

"

Chapter Ten

A Journey of Transformation

I hadn't seen a resume until last night when American dad made one for me in the corner of our studio apartment. It detailed my work history to suggest I had the necessary skills and experience many employers wanted. It included a sales associate helping customers with all the essential information to ease their shopping needs, a human service aide responsible for assisting the physically and mentally disabled clients, and a young, hardworking computer technician accountable for installing computer software. My resume was filled with requirements for many jobs, even though I had yet to lay eyes on one American dollar. Bathed in the soft glow of the table lamp, I looked at my meticulously prepared resume. It was more than just a piece of paper; it was a beacon of hope, a testament to the new beginnings that awaited me in America. I didn't have to worry about whether my experience would be appropriate, whether my English would be perfect, or whether I would be quizzed on all the jobs listed on my resume. My only concern was to do whatever it took to secure employment in America. I was chasing the dream of prosperity, a dream that seemed out of reach just a few months ago.

Much like many Americans, whose knowledge of Africa was mainly based on images of war and starvation, which they saw in movies and National Geographic, or through second-hand information from someone who knew someone who had been to some part of Africa, I also had formed an image of America. I had come to believe that America was synonymous with wealth, beauty, well-fed men and women with potbellies, everyone driving around in brand new cars, living in big houses, and a particular tree growing money for all American citizens.

However, I was taken aback when I learned that America was a land built for those willing to work hard, often juggling two or even three jobs. The notion that your earnings are directly proportional to the number of hours you work in the United States was a revelation. In other words, you are paid by the hour, and the more hours you work, the more you earn. No one is responsible for anyone else; you are solely re-responsible for the life you choose to lead.

Back in Nigeria, I used to yearn for the day when I could shoulder the responsibilities of adulthood and alleviate my parents' struggles. Now, in America, I was determined to succeed, ready to face any challenges that came my way. I was willing to adapt, to learn, and to work in any environment to carve out a path to success.

Two months into my journey, I secured two

jobs — one as a shopping cart pusher at ShopRite and the other as a Sales Floor Associate at Walmart. As a cart pusher, I was the first point of contact for customers, greeting them with a cart as they entered the store. At Walmart, I ensured the shelves were always stocked, helping customers with what they needed and unloading trucks to keep the store replenished. I was a silent hero, making the shopping experience a little easier for everyone.

But my day didn't end there. After my shifts, I would head to Warren County Community College, where I was pursuing a degree in Nursing. I was excited about my education for the first time in a long while. The once familiar sounds of the Jerry Springer show no longer filled my mornings. Instead, the early hours were marked by a newfound sense of purpose — maintaining a B average grade in school. I was no longer a passive observer of daytime television; I was an active participant in my own life.

Despite my busy work schedule, I made sure it didn't interfere with my studies. Twice a week, I attended school, and after classes, I would make my way to the bus stop, my arms laden with textbooks on developmental reading, basic math, sociology, and introductory writing. **Whenever I could, I would sit in the library, immersing myself in my homework.**

"

"The future rewards those who press on. I'm going to press on."

— Barack Obama

"

Chapter Eleven

From Old to New

I woke up in the morning to the wonders of America. Trees were coated with white snow, birds were singing to the start of a new day, dogs were running around in the freshly fallen snow, and excited white children were playing with snowballs. America's bright sun shone radiantly through my window, its warmth melting the bits and pieces of snowfall on the sidewalk. The sweet scent of freshly brewed coffee wafted through the air, a perfect start to a beautiful day. Dressed in a jean suit that complemented my G-Unit sneakers, I felt as if I had seamlessly blended into the American tapestry. The experience of living in America had been nothing short of incredible. The well-constructed amenities and infrastructure made life comfortable and enjoyable.

As I drove to work, I felt a gentle breeze blowing cold air towards the northeast, causing hot vapor to spew out of my mouth as if I were Sango, the god of fire. Despite it being my first winter, I turned on the car heater to keep the inside temperature at ease as I drove past everything on the relatively calm Route 31.

Yet, just six months into my new life in America, I found myself happier than I had ever been. Nigeria, my once beloved homeland, now seemed like a distant memory. With each passing day in America, my affection for my birthplace seemed to diminish. The harsh realities back home were a stark contrast to the life I was now leading. My heart ached at the thought of my mother still living there, amidst the escalating challenges. We keep hoping that things will get better, but they keep getting worse with each passing day.

Stepping into Walmart, I was greeted by a cheerful "Welcome to Walmart" from an elderly gentleman in a blue vest. His warm smile was a stark contrast to the chilly winter air outside. As I moved past shoppers bundled up in their winter coats, I couldn't help but notice the long lines at the checkout counters. Despite only three out of the 22 lanes being open, the customers remained patient, calmly awaiting their turn.

As a Sales Floor Associate at Walmart, earning $7.00 per hour, I found joy in my work. The pay might have been low by American standards, but when converted to Nigerian Naira, it was a substantial amount. In 2006, seven dollars equated to over 1,000 Naira, enough to feed my family for a week. I viewed every expense through the lens of the currency I had left behind.

As soon as I stepped into the bustling environment of Walmart to begin my shift, I was tasked with retrieving shopping carts from the sprawling parking lot.

It was a task that was both physically demanding and mentally taxing. It was like getting paid for a leg workout at the gym, and I often found myself answering questions that seemed obvious, like why the shopping carts were wet after a rainfall.

Venturing outside, I was met with a biting winter breeze. The cold was intense, seeping into my bones and making each step a struggle. The air was so frigid, it felt as if I had stepped into a freezer, the moisture in my breath condensing into tiny clouds that disappeared as quickly as they formed. The parking lot was littered with abandoned carts, their metallic frames gleaming in the winter sun. One by one, I began to collect them, the sound of wheels against asphalt echoing in the crisp air.

Despite wearing my comfortable G-Unit sneakers, the cold was relentless, seeping in through the soles and chilling my feet. I found myself alone in the vast expanse of the parking lot, the realization of the importance of a proper winter attire hitting me hard. This is why people wore winter coats. It wasn't just about fashion or preference; it was a necessity in this freezing weather. My jean jacket and G-Unit sneakers were no match for the winter chill.

As I wrestled with shopping carts in the vast expanse of the Walmart parking lot, a prayer formed in my mind. "Oh God, don't let me die in this parking lot," I pleaded silently. "Please protect me." The words echoed in my head, a mantra against the cold.

The phrase "There's no place like home" took on a whole new meaning as I braved the freezing temperatures, eager to finish my task and return to the warmth of the store.

Suddenly, a voice broke through my thoughts. "Hey, you?" Startled, I looked up to see a white lady beaming with smiles as though she had seen something extraordinary. Was she talking to me? It was a useless, rhetorical question.

It was clear that she was talking to me. She was tall and robust, bundled up in a bulky overcoat, black jeans, a blue hat, and black leather gloves. "Hi, you must be freezing ... Do you need a jacket?" she asked, her voice filled with genuine concern. I was taken aback by her offer, but the biting cold made me nod in agreement. "Yes," I replied, surprised at how quickly I accepted the offer.

I've heard stories about the straightforwardness of white people and their ability to voice their thoughts without hesitation. But experiencing it firsthand was a different matter altogether. The stranger's directness was unexpected, yet it felt refreshing in its own way. She handed me a 3-in-1 black hooded jacket, its warmth seeping into my cold body as I put it on. It was a simple act of kindness, but it meant the world to me at that moment. The warmth of the jacket was not just physical; it was a reminder of the warmth of human kindness, a a beacon of hope in the freezing cold.

"I have been watching you for some time," she said, her voice still filled with concern. "You know it's too cold out here for the little jacket you got on," she added. I nodded in agreement, managing to utter a quiet yes, yes, thank you ... I had thought my jean jacket would be enough for the sunny 40-degree weather, and I hadn't expected to work outside, but due to staff shortages, I was tasked with retrieving shopping carts from the parking lot. She nodded and smiled at me; her eyes unblinking as they met mine. It was as if she understood everything that I had said without me having to explain further. "Okay now ... take care of yourself," she said as she bid me goodbye. "You too, thanks," I replied. Her appearance had erased all the negative feelings I had been experiencing, especially the unappreciated Walmart customers leaving empty **carts all over the parking lot.**

"

"I belong to everybody, and I belong to no-body."

— Muhammadu Buhari

"

Chapter Twelve

Beyond the Job Description

I knew it was over between Walmart and me when I clocked out of my shift. The pain in my feet seemed to have traveled to my back, and I knew I couldn't survive long enough as a cart pusher in freezing rain, scorching sun, and biting winter snow. How much suffering can a young man endure in this country? There would be no more freezing days for me in the parking lot, no more vapor spewing out of my mouth as if I was eating a hot potato. I wanted no more of the never-ending cycle of going on a wild goose chase to bring shopping carts from the parking lot to the store only to have customers take them out to the parking lot again. Never again would I be called to load heavy merchandise into customers' vehicles. I no longer wanted to wear layers of clothing like a madman and no more arriving home sweaty and exhausted. I knew I couldn't keep doing this job. I yearned for a change, for an opportunity that wouldn't leave me physically drained and emotionally spent. It was time to bid farewell to Walmart and embrace new opportunities. It was time for a fresh start, a chance to explore new avenues and discover my true potential in this land of dreams.

I was in the school library, hunched over a bulky Dell computer when my email pinged. The message said, "*What's up? It's me. I have been crying all morning, and it made me happy when I thought of you, so I decided to drop you a line. I was up till 4 a.m., and I finally fixed this retarded computer. I do not know how but I guess I am a miracle worker. It took me a week to do it, though. Anyways, I am having a crappy morning. I wish you would come back to work. I miss having you around. God, I am so depre-*

ssed, and I hope I can get to you because I need you. Oh well, I guess we will talk later!

On several occasions, we had sat down to talk about our lives and events that had happened to us, and I can say I was amazed by how easily she shared her struggles, weaknesses, plans, and intimate details, like how she had three children with three different men. Information I would not have cared to know. I was raised in a culture of secrecy, where we were taught that we don't air out our dirty laundry outside, especially not to strangers. I'd barely known this woman for two weeks.

Her name was Tabitha, but she preferred to be called Tabby. Tabby was the woman who offered me a jacket on that freezing night in the Walmart parking lot. A few days later, she showed up again, this time to check on how I was faring with the new jacket.

"So good to finally see you not freezing!" she exclaimed; her voice sweeter than I remembered. Her red lipstick accentuated her confident smile, a stark contrast to the cold environment around us. However, whenever I thought about reaching out to her, I hesitated. The knowledge of her three children, each from a different father, made me pause.

Her email would have gotten a fast reply if she didn't already have three kids by three different men. It wasn't that I judged her for it; it was just a lot to take in.

It was a Thursday afternoon, as I was making my way to creative writing class, I ran into Alex at the footstep of the first-floor entrance hall, and we engaged in casual conversation. Alex was one of the many white people I sat next to in class, but he was the only one who had chosen me as his partner for our creative writing project. Just as I was about to enter the restroom, I felt a tap on my shoulder. Turning around, I found Alex standing there, and we entered the restroom together.

I turned on the faucet, my reflection staring back at me in front of the wall-to-wall mirror. Out of the corner of my eye. I saw Alex quickly lining up a white powder on a piece of paper. He glanced at me and then around the room, ensuring we were alone. I nodded as if to say no one else was coming.

Is that cocaine?

I wanted to ask. But I didn't feel confident enough to speak up. I looked at Alex's face in the mirror. Two lines of white powder lay on the counter, each as thick as straw and as long as my middle finger. Alex rolled up a one-dollar bill, put his head down to the counter where the powder was, covered one nostril with his finger, and snorted the powder from the other nostril as if he had a cold.

I lowered my hand from my falling jaw which had dropped open in disbelief and returned my gaze to the wood grain surface of the table in front of me. I was at a loss for words. I'd never seen him do anything like this before. Our interactions had always been centered around our creative writing class, discussing plot lines and character development, not ... this. "Here," Alex slid the one dollar across the bathroom counter, I immediately grabbed it without hesitation and shoved it up my nose, sliding it along the line of white powder. I snorted it all up until there was nothing left. It was like I'd done it a hundred times.

"Aaah," I breathed out of my mouth; it was the kind of sigh that comes after a long day or a difficult task, or, in this case, both. Then, I turned to the mirror hanging on the wall, leaning in close to inspect my face. The bathroom light glowed harshly on my skin, highlighting every pore and imperfection. But that wasn't what I was looking for. My gaze was focused on my nose as I turned my head this way and that way to catch a different angle.

With a satisfied nod at my reflection, "Bro,

what was that?" I asked as I stepped back from the mirror.

"It's something to make you feel good, bro," Alex replied. "When we get to class, just sit back and relax,"

As we climbed the two flights of stairs to the classroom on the second floor, I could feel a strange sensation building in my mouth. It was a taste, chemical and nasty, that seemed to materialize out of nowhere. It was like a swift kick at the back of my throat, unexpected and jarring. Despite the odd sensation, I decided not to ask Alex any more questions; the less I knew, the better. *I think I'm starting to prove myself to Alex*, I wondered.

I walked confidently to the front of the class and took a seat. I didn't feel the usual urge to stare at the floor or hide my face. Instead, I was engaging, confident, and full of life. Words flowed from my lips effortlessly, each one hitting its mark with precision.

I was witty and charming, always knowing just what to say to get a laugh or spark a conversation. I had become the class clown, and I reveled in the role. For the first time since coming to America, I didn't worry about my English being perfect or whether my accent would draw unwanted attention. I didn't care if what I said was profound or meaningful. I was just being myself. The two white girls by the exit door seemed captivated by my antics. They no longer saw me as the quiet boy who kept to himself but as someone entirely different: engaging, funny, charming, and witty.

"By the way, my name is Azeez," I said, introducing myself to the group of girls chatting at the school bus stop. They were all my classmates. — Chelsea, Jacquira, and Brenda. Their conversations always seemed lively and full of laughter, and I had often found myself wishing I could be a part of them.

"Yes we know your name," Jacquira replied with a playful chant in her voice.

"Azeez from Africa," Brenda added, pointing at me with a smile. I forced out a smile in return.

"How do you guys like the class so far?" I asked, trying to steer the conversation towards a topic we all had in common.

To my surprise, they all started sharing their thoughts about the class. Chelsea loved the teacher's sense of humor, Jacquira found the lessons interesting, and Brenda was excited about the upcoming midterm project.

My mouth, which usually remained silent, was now engaged in a lively conversation with three gorgeous girls. It was one thing to share a classroom with them; it was an entirely different experience to laugh and chat with them for fifteen minutes on the bus.

After disembarking from the bus, I slipped on my headphones and began the familiar trek towards Railroad Avenue. The music from my Zune player filled my ears, providing a comfortting soundtrack to my journey.

As I was walking, I heard a voice coming from behind me. It was Chelsea. Our eyes locked in a silent exchange; a moment suspended in time. I paused the music on my Zune player, the sudden silence amplifying the anticipation.

"What kind of music are you listening to?" Chelsea called out, her voice cutting through the quiet before she bumped her shoulder against mine in a playful gesture, a spark of camaraderie igniting between us.

"50 Cent," I replied, the words hanging in the air between us.

"I love 50 Cent," she responded enthusiastically. I chuckled softly but said nothing more, expecting her to say goodbye and continue on her way. But she didn't. Instead, she asked me about my experience here in America, her words carrying an undertone of curiosity. "It's nice — I mean, I like it," I responded, a smile spreading across my face. I asked her if she lived nearby, and she nodded in affirmation, adjusting her backpack as she kept pace with me.

I thought about asking her what she was doing following me around but decided it was best not to ask a stupid question. I led her into the main door of my apartment building and then into my living room. She dropped her school bag on the floor with a thud, marking the beginning of an unexpected friendship.

I took a deep breath, watching as Chelsea made herself at home in my one-bedroom apartment. She moved around the space with an ease that suggested familiarity as if she had been here many times before. She casually plucked an orange from the fridge and poured herself a glass of juice, settling comfortably onto a blue couch that I had salvaged from a dumpster just two days ago. One man's trash had indeed become my treasure.

Inspired by her, I walked over to the fridge and poured myself some orange juice. But then, I did something that seemed to shock her.

I added some milk to my orange juice. A look of disgust passed over her face, her nose wrinkling in distaste. It was clear that my unconventional drink choice was not to her liking. But to each their own, I thought, taking a satisfying sip of my creamy citrus concoction.

"You want to try?" I teased, holding out the glass towards her.

She quickly turned her face away, shaking her head vehemently. "That's nasty," she quipped her tone light despite her words. "I'd rather die." *Tonight's supposed to be the big night*, I said to myself, *the night I've dreamed about*. My stomach fluttered with excitement, and my heart revved like an engine.

I sat next to her on the couch, and we got closer and closer. I wrapped my arms around her, barely believing that I could be so lucky. She leaned against me, and as I looked into her eyes, the heat generated between us became too much to resist.

The touch of a white girl on my black skin was all I'd ever wanted, and the raw emotion of the moment brought a lump to my throat. She kissed my neck and reached behind her head with both hands to let her hair down. Then, she held the bottom of her t-shirt and slowly pulled it off.

Her naked body consumed me with emotion as my eyes roamed her body. I put my hands on her shoulder and slid them back to undo her bra. I lowered my head to caress her breast. **My heart was thumping and sweat broke on my brows.**

66

"I was raised to believe that excellence is the best deterrent to racism or sexism. And that's how I operate my life."

— Oprah Winfrey

99

Chapter Thirteen

Triumphs and Trials

May 16th, 2005 marked the beginning of a journey that would prove to be both challenging and rewarding. I was hired as a direct care specialist at a New Jersey state facility for adults with neurodevelopmental disorders. The job title was a fancy way of saying that I would be helping individuals with mental retardation learn life skills. The job came with health benefits, a 401(k) plan, and working hours from 3pm to 11:30pm. However, they failed to mention that the job could also land me in jail. I exuded a cheerful outlook and was enthusiastic about providing proper care for people with mental retardation. I never moaned or frowned when assigned a tough task, such as escorting them to doctor's visits or going to the mall where people would stare as we shopped for clothes and shoes. I did anything anybody wanted me to do just to get along and make nice. I know what it's like to have a conversation with a group of people labeled non-verbal, and I always smile with my coworkers, even when I notice a collective grudge towards me. I channel my time and energy into different ways I can learn from the disabled and provide world-class services to help them do life a little easier. Despite the challenges, I found joy in my work. Every day brought new opportunities to learn and grow, both professionally and personally. And while the job was demanding, it was also incredibly rewarding. Knowing that I was making a difference in the lives of individuals who needed it most made all the hard work worth it.

Wednesday, the day before thanksgiving, I walked into my assigned group of seven individuals with disabilities. Among them was Charles, whose pants were around his knees, leaving him exposed in the middle of the play area. Without a second thought, I rushed over to help him, only to realize that his pants were soaked with urine. As I guided Charles to the bathroom, I heard a *pow*! He suddenly slapped himself on the side of his head. I quickly removed my hand from his shoulder and patted him twice on the back to calm him down. However, Christina, a food service worker, misinterpreted my actions and reported to the supervisor that I had slapped Charles.

Within minutes, the New Jersey Human Services Police arrived at the building. I was astounded at how fast they'd moved on me. In an instant, I went from being a dedicated employee to a potential convict facing serious charges. I was escorted into the supervisor's office by two state police officers.

We sat down and traded stares for a minute. Can we move this along? I thought to myself. Then, one of the police officers opened his notepad. He flipped through it and then looked me in the eye.

"Mr. Azeez. Did I say your name correctly?"

"Yes," I answered.

The officers introduced themselves as Officer James Laycock and Officer Doolittle. "You are being allegedly accused of physically abusing Mr. Charles, a person with developmental disabilities. Mr. Charles is one of the clients you are tasked to provide care for as a direct support professional – is that correct?" he asked.

"Yes, sir," I nodded. A wave of fear washed over me.

"Ms. Christina stated that she witnessed how you slapped S.C. on the back of the head, and our job is to assess the client for any injuries, take pictures, and interview witnesses. If you are found guilty of this crime, you will be charged with endangering the welfare of an incompetent or physically disabled person, a misdemeanor, and second-degree harassment. In addition, injury to a disabled individual is a second-degree felony punishable by two to twenty years in prison and a fine of up to $10,000."

The words hung heavy in the air, my mind filled with confusion and disbelief. I felt deflated, and a wave of anger surged through me. "Sir ...," I heard as I was pulled back from my thoughts. "Is there anything else about what's happened that you would like to add to your statement?"

"Am I going to jail?" I asked, my voice barely above a whisper.

"The truth is, you're a suspect at this point," Officer Doolittle chimed in. In the meantime, you will be sent home on administrative leave, pending the outcome of the investigation. You are free to go pack your things and leave right away."

I left the supervisor's office in a state of shock, I couldn't believe what I just heard. I feel let down by my supervisor who did not say a word, she couldn't vouch for my character and professionalism. I wanted to cry but couldn't. I dragged myself out of the supervisor's office and grabbed my bag with watery eyes and a heavy heart that seemed weighed down with a deadly disease. I left the building without bidding fare well to anyone.

"How is this happening?" No one responded to my question inside the empty car. Now that I feel more comfortable working with individuals with disabilities, this is happening. Now that I have earned their trust and formed a strong bond, this is happening. I had used my body to lift heavy clients out of beds and off toilets, and this is happening. I have learned to communicate with many of them who have been labeled nonverbal. I know when they needed to shower, and I know exactly what I need to do to calm them when they're acting up! Now all of that is at risk. The tears that filled my eyes earlier cascaded down my cheeks. I wept while sitting inside my car.

Hey, you? My phone beeped to announce a new text message. It was from Amanda, pulling me out of my thoughts. *"Are we still hanging out tomorrow?* she wrote. Each time I flirted with Amanda; I vowed it would be the last time. But it never was. I found myself drawn to her. She had a boyfriend, who she said was boring and wasn't satisfying her needs. Or so she claimed.

Didn't you see my messages? More notifications chimed in.

I'm not in a good mood. I tapped out on my cell phone, my fingers moving mechanically over the keypad.

I was reeling from the day's events. The last thing I needed was to get tangled up in Amanda's drama.

Wait, what happened? A new text message is displayed.

I'm sorry. I'm just not in a good mood. I replied.

My phone rang. "What happened? What is wrong with you?" Amanda's voice shouted through the speaker.

"I think I'm going to jail," I said.

"Wait, what? Why? She did not wait for an answer. Oh, no, what did you do? Please talk to me," Amanda pleaded. her voice filled with concern.

"I'm sorry, I don't want to talk about it!"

"What is the problem, Azeez? Please, I'm dying to know."

"I'd rather go home and lay in my bed," I said. "Can you please come and see me right now before my boyfriend get home instead of you being alone and feeling sad?" she offered.

I agreed, hoping that her company would distract me from the day's events. As I put my phone down, I couldn't help but continue to beat myself up over what had happened. The accusations, the police, the potential charges — it all felt like a bad dream. And yet, it was my reality. For now, at least, all I could do was take old exit eleven to Amanda's house.

After driving for twelve minutes, I found her door slightly open. I let myself in, the familiarity of the place offering some comfort. "Hey, thanks for having me. I appreciate it," I said, making my way to the couch where she was sitting.

"I didn't think we planned on seeing each other today." I said, a hint of surprise in my voice. She looked at me, a playful smile on her face.

"What can I say? I find you irresistible at times," she replied. "Heineken?"

"Sure." I took a swallow of the beer.

"So, tell me what happened," Amanda quickly replied. "I cannot believe someone could make such an allegation against me; how could she do this to me? How could she act so friendly and then stab me in the back like that?" Amanda listened. "I know I'm not the best at showing up to work on time due to an hour-long drive from school on weekdays, but I was never late more than fifteen minutes. And when I was, I always called my supervisors beforehand ..."

"Azeez, look, offering her own perspective on the situation. "Don't let the fake smiles of these white people fool you and their seemingly friendly conversations. They're a bunch of bitches, yo." I nodded in agreement. "How about we smoke weed, and you forget your sorrows?" she suggested.

I smiled at her suggestion. Despite the turmoil of the day, we passed a blunt back-and-forth as I found solace in our conversation. Moments like these made our unexpected meetings worthwhile. The comfort of Amanda's company, the ease of our conversations, and the undeniable connection we shared provided a much-needed respite from my troubles. But as the saying goes, all good things must come to an end. I was able to forget my troubles. But my time is up.

As I walked out, Amanda's voice trailed behind me. "I hope you feel a little better," she said.

"Yes, thank you so much," I replied, my hand resting on the doorknob. I adjusted my pants and took one last look at Amanda before stepping out into the night.

The drive home was quiet, the only sound being the hum of the car engine providing a soothing backdrop to my thoughts. My phone buzzed intermittently, lighting up the dark interior of the car with incoming text messages. Amanda's words flashed across the screen, a reminder of the connection we shared, and the occasional buzz of my phone.

"Wanna know what I'm thinking?" She did not wait for me to reply. *"I'm thinking about you having your way with me and how much I'm gonna enjoy it."* A new text chimed in.

Tomorrow, I want you to fuck me standing, sitting, and bent over from the back.

Please don't be shy because I intend on having a really good time with you, another text announced.

I'm kind of a freak in bed. How's that? The messages don't stop. *You're seriously too cute, and I have something in mind that I plan to wear tomorrow just for you.*

The night was dark, but the stars were out in full force, their light a comforting presence in the vast expanse of the sky. I snapped my flip phone shut, a smile spreading across my face as I drove. I was in a good mood. Amanda's words, laughter, and presence had drawn me in like a moth to a flame. **I had never felt so connected to another person.**

"

"If I were to say, 'God, why me?' about the bad things, then I should have said, 'God, why me?' about the good things."

— Arthur Ashe

"

Chapter Fourteen

Crossing Horizons

I woke up early on the morning of Thanksgiving, a day American people pause and give thanks for their blessings and freedoms. I found myself filled with appreciation for my friendship with Amanda, a beacon of light in the midst of my turmoil, and I looked forward to our first rendezvous. Despite my best efforts, the word "jail" kept intruding upon my thoughts, casting a shadow over the day. Yet, I propelled myself forward the morning after the news. *Did I really slap him?* The voice in my head was relentless. *"It's over. You are a prisoner now."* The image of my hands bound and the sound of a cell door opening was chillingly vivid. But I refused to accept it.

I clung to the truth that I knew — I would never intentionally harm anyone. The accusation was absurd. *"I am innocent for the love of God ...,* I did not do what she said I did." I had dedicated myself to the care of these people, changing their diapers two to three times a shift, transporting them in wheelchairs, soothing tantrums, and providing comfort in their most vulnerable moments. I had proven my dedication and responsibility time and again. My patience had been tested, my honesty questioned, my commitment challenged, and yet, I remained steadfast. I had borne the brunt of physical assaults — spat at, kicked, punched, and scratched — and never for once retaliated. I had performed tasks that many would balk at —cleaning mucus from trachea tubes, emptying and cleaning colostomy bags so often that I'd lost count. It was a role I embraced with compassion and understanding, knowing the immense trust placed in me.

The injustice of it all shook me to my core as I sat in silence, waiting for a call from the State Police.

"I get this nervous feeling ... I don't know; it's weird. It's not the situation that makes me nervous; it's you. I don't know why but you do. That's the weird thing because I'm not the nervous type."

I took a deep breath as I opened Amanda's Facebook messages. We had a rule – we do not text during the day since she's a girl with a boyfriend, and we needed to tread carefully. Instead, we used Facebook to talk about everything we vowed to do to each other throughout the day. In a flash, all the thoughts of potential arrest were released from my head like air escaping from a balloon. The world fell silent for a few moments as I absorbed her words.

"I can't stop thinking about you. I think about your arms wrapped around me, holding

me close." A sigh slipped past my lips as I began to type my response. "I just love everything about you," my fingers moved over the keys with a familiarity born of countless conversations. I knew that in a few hours, the girl whose love had given me a reason to smile would be in my bed.

"Just being around you makes me happy, and I love everything about you, too. You are an incredible person and very easy to talk to. I could tell you anything and it would stay between us. I'm glad that we got to know each other, and I care about you a lot, she responded-ed.

In that moment, all the chaos and uncertainty seemed to fade into the background. It was just us — two people connected by words and shared dreams. A grin spread across my face in the solitude of my room; "happiness" was too mild a word to describe the euphoria that surged through me. The anticipation of seeing Amanda, the girl whose love had given me a reason to smile, was overwhelming.

As the afternoon wore on, I found myself checking my breath and spraying AXE body spray all over. The fragrance filled the room, serving as a tangible reminder of the impending rendezvous.

"Be there in 15 minutes." The beep of my phone broke the silence. It was a text from Amanda, and my heart skipped a beat at her words.

Around 6:30 p.m., the soft knock on the door of apartment 107B signaled her arrival. As I swung the door open, she immediately lifted her shirt up and burst out, "Surprise motherfucker!" Laughter echoed between us and two beautiful bouncing breasts stared at me.

We didn't exchange any pleasantries — no handshake no inquiry about how the day had been. Instead, I extended my hand to clasp hers, my other arm encircling her waist. I drew a deep breath, the scent of her freshly washed hair filling my senses. It was a smell I knew well, one that brought a sense of comfort and familiarity. The world beyond the confines of the apartment faded into insignificance as I guided her into the bedroom.

She made herself comfortable on the bed, a relaxed ease in her posture. "Who would have known that I would like a Black dude so much!" she exclaimed, her voice filled with genuine surprise and affection. "Maybe it was your accent that did the trick, but maybe it was more than just that, which I can't exactly put my finger on."

I couldn't help but smile at her words. "Are you telling me that I'm your first?" I asked, a playful grin on my face.

"Well, you are the first Black dude I have ever let inside me. Your accent turns me on, and seriously, I don't know what it is about you, but you really do it for me."

Her face glowed with a subtle satisfaction as she spoke, her words sincere and heartfelt. As she rose from the bed, I watched her, and my mind filled with thoughts of our shared connection and **the unique bond we had formed.**

"

"Sometimes you look back at girls you spent money on rather than send it to your mom, and you realize witchcraft is real."

— Robert Mugabe

"

Chapter Fifteen

Crossroads of Consequence

After another day passed without a single phone call from the police, the silence of my phone served as a stark reminder of the looming uncertainty that hung over me like a dark cloud. Then, unexpectedly, it rang. The voice on the other end was soft, almost a whisper, "Hi, can I please speak with Azeez Akande?" "Yes, Ma'am. This is Azeez," I replied, striving to keep my voice steady.

"My name is Chelsea Parker, a quality assurance officer with the state of New Jersey ..." Her words sent a jolt of panic through me. I felt my breath hitch in my throat as she continued, "I've been assigned to your case, and I would like for us to meet and discuss it." My heart felt as if it was being torn apart. The fear was so palpable it felt as if I was on the verge of a heart attack.

This woman, a stranger to me, held the reins of my future. In just a few hours, she would decide the trajectory of my life. The thought of losing my job and facing incarceration filled me with dread. With a heavy heart, I made my way to my car and embarked on the drive to the state capitol building. The journey seemed to stretch on forever, each minute ticking by slower than the last.

Upon arriving at the imposing structure of the capitol building, I couldn't help but wonder what lay ahead. Would this mark the end of everything I had worked so hard for? Or could it possibly herald a new beginning? Only time would reveal the answers.

"Good morning," I greeted the secretary in the lobby. My voice echoed slightly in the vast space. "My name is Azeez Akande, and I am here for Chelsea Parker." "Mr. Akande, come on in........."

Thanks for coming out to talk to me on short notice." Officer Parker welcomed me, her voice steady and professional. We shook hands, a formal exchange in an otherwise informal world. She closed the door behind us, sealing us off from the rest of the building. "How are you doing?" she asked, her tone softening slightly. The question hung in the air. It had been tough, to say the least. I took a seat, maintaining eye contact with her. My arms were folded across my chest, a subconscious protective gesture. My head was bent to the side, as if trying to shield myself from the impending conversation.

Officer Parker's gaze was unwavering as she delved into the crux of the matter. "The parents of the client, States Charles, are very active in the oversight of the health and well-being of their son. Christina provided a statement that you, Mr. Azeez, slapped Mr. Charles on the back of the head, which is corroborated by Ms. Pickens and Mr. Dugger (Exhibit M-5). As you are aware, how you perform your job must conform to the standards for the rights of the developmentally disabled performance agreement. Courtesy and respect are always demonstrated by all employees when dealing with clients, fellow employees, and the public."

Her words were direct, leaving no room for ambiguity. "Your responsibilities also state, any form of communication, which is or could be considered insulting, sexually suggestive, derogatory, discourteous, or defamatory towards others, will not be tolerated and all employees are to clearly understand that such unacceptable communication will result in appropriate corrective, administrative, or disciplinary action."

The weight of her words hung in the air like a heavy fog. The allegations were serious and carried significant consequences. I knew this was not merely a meeting; it was a crossroads that could drastically alter my life's path. The hearing officer's verdict was clear and unequivocal.

"It is the hearing officer's opinion that through a preponderance of the evidence, management has met the burden of proof for all charges; discourtesy to the public, visitors, patients, or residents (C20.1), N.J.A.C 4A:2- 2.3(a)6 Conduct unbecoming a public employee; N.J.A.C. 4A:2-2.3a)11 Other sufficient cause," she declared.

She went on to explain that all witnesses observed, and I admitted that I placed my hand at the back of client S.C.'s neck when guiding him to the restroom, which was deemed unacceptable. Moreover, failing to ensure that the client's pants were pulled up before prompting him to move forward was considered unsafe as the client could have toppled forward with my hand still on his neck.

"I wasn't sure I heard you correctly, ma'am. Did you say all charges were upheld?" I queried; my voice barely audible.

"Exactly. That's correct," she affirmed. Tears welled up in my eyes as I asked, "Now what?"

"As to the penalty...," she commenced, and I braced myself for the impending revelation. The range for the first-time infraction of the C-20 charge is an official reprimand and a five day suspension."

"Five days suspension," I echoed, disbelief evident in my voice.

"Yes, considering it could be worse," she stated matter-of-factually.

I nodded in response, trying to digest the unfolding events.

"Management issued the highest penalty within the range..." she continued.

Her words began to blur at this point. All I could focus on was the five-day suspension. It seemed so trivial compared to the potential alternatives.

"Your suspension without pay has been lifted, and you're allowed to return to work tomorrow. You'll receive a letter for the five-day suspension, which you can then accept or file an appeal with your union representative if you disagree," she concluded.

We shook hands and said our goodbyes. As I exited her office, a wave of relief washed over me.

It was over ... at least for now.

66

"The best way to not feel hopeless is to get up and do something."

— Obama

99

Chapter Sixteen

Navigating the Corridors of Pain

Life had been normal; work, home and the occasional night out. Then came the pain. A persistent ache in my chest that wouldn't go away. The doctor had been vague, suggesting it could be anything from a pulled muscle to arthritis. But as days turned into weeks, and the pain became a constant companion, I knew it was something more serious. The drive to Saint Luke's Family Practice was a haze; the familiar landmarks along Route 31 South seemed distant, as if I was seeing them through a thick fog. Nurse Becky, with her kind smile and reassuring manner, tried to put me at ease as she guided me through the maze-like corridors of the hospital. "One-twenty over eighty. It's perfect," she said, after checking my blood pressure in the glass-walled exam room. But her words did little to calm my racing heart.

The thumping footsteps echoed in the sterile silence of the exam room as Dr. Jack knocked on the door. "Come in," I said, my voice barely above a whisper. He entered, a friendly smile on his face as he introduced himself. We exchanged pleasantries, discussing everything from my heritage to his friend's mission trip to Africa. But all I could think about was the pain in my chest, the constant companion that had made itself at home in my body over the past few months.

"So, you are having chest pain?" He finally asked, his tone shifting from casual to professional. I nodded, explaining how it came and went, a dull ache that seemed to radiate from deep within my chest. He examined me thoroughly, his stethoscope cold against my skin as he listened to my breathing and checked my vitals.

"On a scale of one to ten, what's your pain level?" he asked.

"Seven," I replied, pointing to the area where the pain was most intense. He nodded, scribbling something on his notepad before prescribing me Naproxen and ordering a chest x-ray.

Despite following his instructions in the letter, my condition did not improve. In fact, it seemed to worsen. I lost weight and the pain persisted. Desperate for answers, I returned to Dr. Jack.

"It might be HIV-related," he said, his words hitting me like a punch in the gut. I stared at him in disbelief, shaking my head as if that could somehow erase what he'd just said. But there it was, written on the lab prescription in his hand: "HIV test."

"Dr. Jack," I began,

"I've been thinking ... Maybe I just bent the wrong way at work. Or perhaps the pain will go away on its own. It could be arthritis, right?"

Dr. Jack looked at me, his expression unreadable. I could see him weighing my words, considering the possibilities. "I understand your concerns," he said finally. "And it's possible that the pain could be due to a physical strain or arthritis. But given your symptoms and their persistence, it's important that we rule out all possibilities, including HIV." I nodded, understanding his point but still feeling a knot of fear in my stomach. The thought of undergoing an HIV test was terrifying, but I knew it was necessary.

"Let's take it one step at a time," Dr. Jack suggested. "We'll start with the test and go from there. Remember, no matter what the results are, we're here to support you and help you through it."

As I sat in my Hyundai Sonata, the sterile smell of the hospital still lingering in my nostrils, I looked down at the piece of paper clutched in my trembling hand. The words written on it seemed to blur and swim before my eyes.

Of all the things that could scare me, this was the most horrendous one. "What kind of shit is this?" I whispered to myself; the words barely audible over the hum of the car's engine. The drive home was a blur. The world outside seemed distant and unreal as I tried to process what I'd just been told. The thought of being tested for HIV was terrifying, but I knew it was something I had to face. But not today. Today, I needed time to prepare myself mentally for what lay ahead.

As soon as I reached home, I threw myself onto my bed, the plastic bag I was holding discarded onto a chair. The world seemed to spin around me as I buried my face into the pillow, my mind a whirlwind of fear and uncertainty. Sleep came unexpectedly, a brief respite from the torment of my thoughts. But it was short-lived. I woke up in a cold sweat, the reality of my situation crashing down on me like a tidal wave.

The digital numbers on my alarm clock glowed in the darkness, indicating that it was four in the morning. Sleep eluded me as I lay there, staring at the ceiling. The questions that had been plaguing me since Dr. Jack's revelation came rushing back. What if I had HIV? Could I recover from it? What would my father say? The questions swirled around in my head, making me dizzy with fear and anxiety.

Despite the turmoil within me, I managed to drag myself out of bed and headed to the lab. The journey felt like an eternity, each second stretching out as I repeated a silent prayer over and over again. "Please let me not have HIV. God, please let me not have AIDS."

The wait at Lab Corp on Washington Avenue was agonizing. Each tick of the clock seemed to echo my pounding heart as I waited for my turn. The man who took my blood was impassive, his face giving away nothing as he went about his task with practiced efficiency.

"When will I get the results?" I asked, trying to keep my voice steady.

"In 2-4 weeks," he replied, his voice devoid of any emotion. "You can check with your doctor for the preliminary result after two weeks."

As I stepped out of the lab, a sense of emptiness washed over me. I tried to come to terms with what lay ahead.

Back at home, I opened my closet and my eyes landed on a grey shirt — a painful reminder of that fateful night in Atlantic City. A night that might have changed everything. **A night that might have opened the door to this terrifying possibility.**

"

"Your experience will be a lesson to all of us men to be careful not to marry ladies in very high positions."

— Idi Amin

"

Chapter Seventeen

An Unforgettable Casino Night

My train of thought was cut short as I remembered all the baffling things that I had experienced during the weekend getaway to Atlantic City with Emily. From the moment we set foot in the city, I was consumed with a single thought how to impress her. Emily, my charming friend from work, had invited me to accompany her to the casino, an invitation I accepted without a second thought. Not only was it my first time visiting a casino, but also a golden opportunity to spend quality time with Emily, whose beauty was only surpassed by her captivating personality. I remember dressing up in a grey shirt, blue jeans, and a pair of no-name sneakers from Walmart. I wanted to look my best for her. After all, we were there to have fun.

Our first night in Atlantic City was nothing short of magical. We indulged in a couples' massage, got our nails done, and even tried our luck at the slot machines. Although we both lost a hundred dollars, the thrill of the game and the shared laughter more than made up for it. It wasn't about the games; it was about creating memorable moments with Emily. As the night wore on, we found ourselves at Jay-Z's 40/40 club. Surrounded by the pulsating music and the vibrant crowd, we drank and laughed until midnight. And every time I looked at Emily, her smile told me I was succeeding in impressing her. Her eyes sparkling with excitement and joy, I couldn't help but wonder what the future held for us.

The night back at the hotel was a whirlwind of passion and desire. She began unbuttoning her shirt, exposing her lace bra. Our eyes locked, and there was an unspoken understanding between us. I watched her closely as she slid her mesh bikini-style panties off. It was like a race to see who could get undressed quicker. I moved closer to her; I gently wrapped my arm around her waist as I undid my pants. I sighed as she sat on top of me. My eyes were closed, and the world outside ceased to exist as we lost ourselves in the moment.

But then, something unexpected happened. I felt something strange between my thighs.

Emily's voice broke through my daze, her concern evident. "Are you okay?" she asked.

Before I could answer; I felt a wave of panic wash over me.

I rushed to the bathroom, my mind racing. Emily's voice echoed from outside the door, her words barely registering as I tried to make sense of what was happening. I couldn't see well enough to make out what was between my legs. "I am so sorry...

I wasn't expecting my period ..." she said. Her words hit me like a punch in the gut.

I didn't have to look down to know I needed more water.

Are you okay? Without waiting for a response, Emily approached the bathroom door, pausing before knocking, but I was too lost in my thoughts to respond. The reality of the situation was beginning to sink in.

I need to go home, I yelled, the sound of the shower water drowning out my words. The thought of Emily's blood on me was too much to bear.

In hindsight, I realized that I should have worn a condom. But in the heat of the moment, blinded by lust and hormones, I had thrown caution to the wind. I had ignored the potential dangers of unprotected sex, too caught up in the moment to consider the consequences. Now, I was facing the possibility that I might have contracted HIV from Emily.

The realization hit me like a ton of bricks. It was a harsh wake-up call, a reminder of my foolishness and ignorance. I had prioritized sexual pleasure over my well-being, and now I was paying the price.

That evening, I found myself glued to my desktop, desperately searching for answers on Google. The more I read about HIV symptoms, the more helpless and stupid I felt. But there was no one else to blame but myself.

The rest of the day passed in a blur. Nightmares plagued my sleep, each one more terrifying than the last. Each morning, I would wake up in a cold sweat, clutching my chest as if trying to ease the pain that seemed to radiate from within. Despite everything, there was a part of me that refused to give up hope. Perhaps it was some sort of curse from Nigeria or just a cruel twist of fate. But whatever it was, I knew that I had to face it head-on. With a heavy heart, I got up from my bed and decided to go for a walk, hoping that it would help clear my mind.

As I walked down the road toward railroad

avenue, every passing glance from a stranger felt like an accusation, a silent judgment. Could they tell just by looking at me? Could my father tell? Could the couple walking on the other side of the road read me? Is that why they crossed over to the other side just now? The questions plagued me, gnawing at my sanity.

I found solace in the tranquility of a lake that had caught my eye on the way. The environment was peaceful and comforting, with the addition of a slight breeze. I forgot about everything as I lay back on the grass under the shade of a tree and enjoyed what I was given. I was captivated by the sight of waves dancing on the river's surface in front of me. It was beautiful, alluring, and almost addicting. I stared at the soothing presence of those waves playing tag with each other, and before I knew it, I was standing at the edge. It felt so relaxing just to stand there and stare at my reflection. I wondered if it was too cold for a swim. It felt so smooth to look at, I wanted to feel it against my entire skin. So, I shifted forward, and after rolling my pants up to my knees, I let my legs drop and dive into the water. It was not too cold, just perfect. I liked it. I swung my legs over the surface of the water, letting my feet dip slightly as I did so. Unbelievably good. It had a homier feeling than my home. For a moment, I allowed myself to forget, to lose myself in the beauty of nature. But the peace was short-lived.

The memory of that night came rushing back, shattering the calm. The sight of blood, the fear, the uncertainty — it all came crashing down on me. I felt exposed and vulnerable. Every glance felt like an accusation, every whisper a condemnation. I sat there, huddled on the shore, my knees drawn up to my chest. The world around me seemed distant and unreal. I was lost in my thoughts, trapped in a nightmare that seemed to have no end. I don't know how long I sat there, staring blankly at the rippling water.

Time seemed to stand still, each second stretching out into an eternity. But eventually, reality came crashing back. I realized that I had lost track of time. With a heavy heart, I got up and began to walk back home. Each step felt like a struggle, a battle against the overwhelming tide of fear and uncertainty.

The early morning light painted the sky in hues of orange and pink as I woke up the next day, a sight I hadn't seen in a while. Over the weeks, my routine had changed drastically. I found myself staring blankly at the ceiling for hours before finally mustering the energy to get up and prepare for work. My appetite had dwindled, and I found myself eating only once or twice every two days. A banana, a few biscuits, half a cup of milk, or sometimes just a few candies felt like more than enough. Getting dressed for work became a challenge. The mere thought of opening my closet felt like stepping on a bed of nails.

I managed to grab a shirt with my eyes lowered, hoping it would be suitable for work. But when I opened my eyes and saw that I was holding the grey shirt, I felt a surge of panic. I quickly threw it under the bed before grabbing another shirt and rushing out of the house.

Some might perceive my behavior as an overreaction, but how can they truly understand? How can anyone grasp the turmoil of savoring life's joys one moment, only to be confronted with a potential disgrace to one's family or nation the next? This was my reality. My actions would not only cast a shadow over my family but also over my entire race. People may generalize that every African is like me. And why? Because of the reckless actions of a naive boy, driven by lust rather than common sense. A fortunate village boy who had the rare opportunity to go to America, only to squander it by contracting HIV. I was consumed by fear, and rightfully so. I was entitled to my fear, for it was a chilling reflection of the grim reality I faced.

The ensuing days unfolded in a monotonous rhythm, each one indistinguishable from the last. However, a subtle shift began to occur after spending countless hours by the water's edge, my toes idly skimming the surface. The water seemed to call out to me, its gentle lapping against the shore whispering an invitation. At first, the pull was faint, but as the days turned into a week, it grew stronger. A voice in my head echoed its plea, urging me to surrender to the water's embrace.

Two days before the test results were due, I found myself grappling with a profound loss of will to live. I felt like a discarded piece of trash, my health and well-being relegated to the bottom of my priority list. I was acutely aware of the disgrace I had brought upon my family and my race. My actions had painted a damning picture for all to see and judge. I was a fool who had let lust cloud his judgment, who had failed to consider the potential consequences of his actions. I felt undeserving of life itself. The voice in my head grew louder, its calls more insistent. It promised a peaceful end, a chance to slip away quietly rather than face the harsh reality of my actions.

With this grim resolution in mind, I returned home. I decided to pack up my belongings and give away what others could use. Despite knowing it wouldn't change anything, I wanted to leave behind something good. I spent most of the night sorting through my things and even cooked a traditional African dish for my father. I called my mother and told her I loved her. Exhausted, I eventually fell into a fitful sleep and woke up feeling strangely at peace the next day. I had come to terms with my fate and was ready to face whatever lay ahead.

The ring of my phone broke the silence I was enjoying. It was the doctor's office calling to inform me that my test results were ready for collection. The news hit me like a ton of bricks — it felt like an intrusion, an unwelcome interruption in my carefully laid plans. My heart skipped a beat.

Despite the fear gnawing at me, I knew that I had to collect the results. If left uncollected, it could potentially expose the secret that I was desperately trying to hide. Today was about finding peace and acceptance amidst the chaos. With a sense of urgency, I took a shortcut to the hospital, saving precious minutes. I navigated the familiar hallways with a brisk pace, descended into the elevator, and crossed the fancy lobby with a composed demeanor.

The receptionist asked me for my name and date of birth, which I provided. She then turned around, rummaged through a tray filled with similar envelopes, and handed one over to me. With the sealed envelope in hand, I thanked her and left without any further conversation.

I felt a slight sigh escape my lips as I hurried home and placed the sealed envelope on the table. I already had a good idea of what it would say. Why should I ruin my mood by confirming what I feared? I finished packing and grabbed my bag, ready to go. But as I was heading for the door, my gaze fell where the envelope lay untouched. I couldn't help but stare at it for a while, feeling a surge of curiosity. I wanted to know for sure, even if it hurt. So, I snatched the envelope, ripped it open eagerly, and unfolded the papers. I scanned the first page and saw nothing surprising. It was just my blood count, which was normal. The second page also had some irrelevant data. The third and final page had only one thing written on it.

I almost forgot how to breathe.

JOURNEY TO AMERICA

Acknowledgments

—

I give all glory to God for His guidance and protection through my days of joy and sorrow. I am deeply grateful to the wonderful people of America, to whom I owe so much. My profound gratitude goes to Senator Edward Kennedy, whose tireless efforts in passing the Immigration Act of 1990 brought me to the United States; I offer him a heartfelt thank you.

This book represents my endeavor to unveil the world from which I emerged and offer a candid narrative of my life's journey as I recollect it. My father, Sikiru Akande, opened mighty doors for me, and for that, I am eternally grateful. My mother, Elizabeth Akande, deserves special thanks for her unending prayers.

About the Book

—

I nurtured an audacious dream as a twelve-year-old in a humble African village. It was a dream that society deemed inappropriate for someone of my age and circumstances to experience an intimate connection with a woman from a different continent, specifically, a Caucasian woman from America. This dream was more than just a youthful fantasy; it represented my desire to transcend boundaries and experience life beyond the confines of my village.

Despite the odds stacked against me, I held onto this dream with unwavering determination. I invested time and effort into transforming this seemingly impossible dream into a tangible reality. This book is a testament to that journey and is meant to inspire anyone who dares to dream beyond their current situation.

About the Author

Azeez Akande, a Nigerian-born immigrant and a graduate of Kean University, is an author who prides himself on his excellent communication skills, both in writing and listening. Young, vibrant, and persistent in his goals, Azeez is a testament to the power of determination and perseverance.

His journey to America is an incredible story that he hopes will inspire others. The people he met along the way shaped every step of his journey, every challenge he faced, and every success he achieved. Their influence has been a guiding light in his life. Among these individuals are people with intellectual and developmental disabilities. Their presence in his life introduced him to a kinder perspective on life, teaching him the value of empathy and understanding.

Today, Azeez Akande lives in Indiana with his wife and three children. His experiences have shaped him into the man he is today. A man who values communication, persistence, and kindness. Through his writing, he hopes to share these values with others and inspire them on their own journeys.

For speaking engagement bookings, please contact:

Email: azeezakande@yahoo.com

Facebook.com/azeezakande

Instagram.com/azeezakande

Some of the Challenges Azeez Faced in America

1. **Cultural Differences:** Adapting to a new culture can be difficult. Everything from social norms and customs to food and language can be vastly different from what one is used to.

2. **Language Barrier:** Difficulties in communication. Mastering a new language is a significant challenge for many immigrants.

3. **Employment:** Finding a job in a new country can be tough, especially without local references or recognition of foreign qualifications.

4. **Homesickness:** Being far from family, friends, and familiar surroundings can lead to isolation and loneliness.

5. **Discrimination:** Unfortunately, immigrants often face discrimination, which can affect many aspects of their lives, from finding housing and employment to their mental health.

Some of the Successes Azeez Achieved in America

1. **Education:** Azeez graduated from Kean University, which is a significant achievement. Higher education often provides better job opportunities and is a common goal for many immigrants.

2. **Communication Skills:** Azeez prides himself on his excellent communication skills in writing and listening. Mastering a new language to the point of being an effective communicator is a considerable success.

3. **Family:** Azeez lives in Indiana with his wife and three children. Establishing a family and providing for them in a new country is a significant accomplishment.

4. **Authoring a Book:** Writing and publishing a book is no small feat. It requires dedication, discipline, and hard work. By authoring "Journey to America," Azeez has shared his story and contributed to the literature on immigrant experiences.

5. **Influence and Inspiration:** Through his book, Azeez hopes to inspire others who may be embarking on their own journeys. Being able to influence and inspire others is a remarkable achievement.